Triumph of the Spirit, Triumph of the Mind

MEMOIRS
Of A

Learning Disabled, Dyslexic
MULTIMILLIONAIRE

Allen Weinstein

Copyright © 2015 Allen Weinstein.
All rights reserved
First Edition

PAGE PUBLISHING, INC.
New York, NY

First originally published by Page Publishing, Inc. 2015

ISBN 978-1-68139-471-8 (pbk)
ISBN 978-1-68139-472-5 (digital)

Printed in the United States of America

Dedicated to my

mom and dad,

Kitty and Morris Weinstein

Dedicated to my

mom and dad,

Kitty and Morris Weinstein

While completing this book, I had lost one of my brothers, my best friend, and my business partner.

I know he is with our parents looking down on me; I dedicate this book in his memory as well.

"Joe, your spirit will live on through all the lives you have touched."

My other brother Warren currently lives in California. Warren certainly has a fighting spirit. He has always had a love for flying and was so committed that he drove a truck to pay for flying lessons. Determined to achieve this goal he entered the Air Force Academy where he graduated as an officer and became a pilot in the United States Air Force. After completing his military service he went on to become a Captain for American Airlines. He's now retired and enjoys spending quality time as a grandfather. Warren, thanks for all of your loving support through the years.

Contents

About the Author 9
To My Readers 13
My Letter to a Stranger 15
Acknowledgments 17
Chelsea School Keynote Graduation Speech 21

Part 1: Synopsis of My Life 30
Losing It 31
The FDIC 47
Long Beach 55
School Days 71
Making It 88
Sweet Smell of Success 104

Part 2: Prescription for a Successful Life 120
Power 121
Prescription for a Successful Life 127
Control Your Future 132
Imagery 135
The Brain: Conscious, Subconscious 142
Preconditioning 151
Healing 156
The Computer 159

The Brain: A Microprocessor 163
Labeling 167
Misguided Use of Brainpower
    The Need for Reprogramming Brains 176
The Disease of Rehabilitation or the Lack Thereof 181
Change: The Key to Self-Satisfaction 184
Helping Others Requires Changes Within 188

Conclusion 193
A Personal Vision 196

About the Author

Today, Allen Weinstein is a self-made man, a man who acquired success in life despite handicaps that might have left him a street derelict. In the crucible of our public education system, Allen had never been given much of a chance to succeed. Failure after failure in school sentenced him to a bleak future. Yet Allen found a way to deal with the blows life dealt him and a way to overcome his particular handicaps. He forged a philosophy of life from his experiences that has carried him through the darkest of times to ultimate triumph. In this book, *Memoirs of a Learning-Disabled, Dyslexic Multimillionaire*, Allen tells his story and shares his lessons from life. From the streets of a small beach town in Long Island, New York, to meetings with the movers and shakers of our society, Allen takes us on his journey from a virtual unknown to a man of means and power. For anyone who has despaired about the difficulties life has handed out to him, for anyone who wants to discover how to triumph over adversity, this is the book to read.

ABOUT THE AUTHOR

Nobody believed Allen Weinstein was college material except Allen himself, therefore he shocked everyone around him by getting accepted and attending Tulane University and through his alternative methods of learning Allen also attended Columbia university night school and finally graduated from the university of Kansas where he received his degree in architecture. As a founding partner of Unity Capital Corporation, he was instrumental in its phenomenal growth and development as a major player in the real estate markets of the northeast. Allen is a health aficionado and enjoys working out along with golf, tennis, and skiing. He also enjoys creating art and sculpture. He has written three beautifully illustrated books showing some of his creative projects. The most spectacular of which is a doll house that took him thirteen years to complete.

Allen has worked with various charities and numerous politicians. Such work has netted charities like the Mental Illness Foundation a $100,000 grant from New York State, in addition to the tens of thousands of dollars he personally raised each year at various charity dinners.

MIF RECEIVES $100,000 GRANT FROM NYS

The Mental Illness Foundation is proud to announce that it has received a grant of $100,000 from the State of New York. The funds were awarded due to the efforts of MIF Board member Allen Weinstein, and state senator Norman J. Levy.

Allen Weinstein

The grant has been earmarked to be used to develop a family outreach project to help the mentally ill and their families in Nassau County. MIF will work with the Mental Health Association of Nassau County in setting up a Center for Families of the Mentally Ill.

The purpose of this special center is to encourage families with mentally ill members to reach out for guidance, support and resource data, as they learn to cope with the devastating effects of mental illness. The Center will provide phone help lines 365 days a year. Social workers will be available to help family members. And a special Outreach Unit will be established, so that social workers can go directly into the home to provide assistance for the mentally ill living with their families.

MIF is grateful to Senator Levy, and the State of New York for helping us to help the mentally ill.

To My Readers

This book is written in two parts. Part one is a synopsis of my life. It describes all the educational *handicaps* I have and how my personal and business life have been affected by *the trials and tribulations* I endured while growing up and while meeting the challenges of the business world.

Part Two, "Prescription for a Successful life," describes my theories and insights into creating a triumphant life. It will give you, the reader, a clear view of how I changed a *potentially failed* life into one of health, happiness, love, and financial success.

My Letter to a Stranger

A stranger passed through my life for a fleeting moment. His life will continue without a second thought of ever having met me, but to me, he was no stranger. To me he was an angel who appeared at the scene of an accident to offer much needed help and comfort. Strangers crossing each other's paths at the exact time of need are a destiny too complex to unravel. Little did this stranger know that his destiny that day was to be my angel. Without his generous help and comforting ways, my unfortunate experiences could have been a nightmare instead of a cherished memory.

We are all emissaries of love and compassion. Sometimes during our harried schedules of life, we lose focus, but this was your moment to grow wings and become my angel, and then like all angels, pass out of my life as mysteriously as you entered! I am certain you have forgotten what you have done by now, angels often do, but I never will. Thank you.

Every one of us at one time or another has had our chance to grow wings and become someone's angel. We just do not think of it as a spiritual experience. Maybe if we did, we would begin to realize we are all emissaries of a higher being, even if that being is only within ourselves.

Acknowledgments

First, Mom and Dad, thank you for passing on to me your love, wisdom, and perception. This trifecta of treasures and your spirit continue to give all of those in our family guidance each day of our lives. I love you.

Thanks to Nellie, my nanny, my tutor, and my best friend, who raised me and met my every need. She was always there, and I loved being with her. God knows, I was not easy to deal with.

Thanks to my daughters, Sherri and Dana, for their love, devotion, understanding, and continued encouragement. You have given to me a new and wonderful family of sons, grandchildren, and in-laws for which I am eternally grateful. You are the beacons of my life, the heart of my soul, and the reason why I am the richest man in the world; and as you have continued to grow and to achieve in your chosen paths of life, you have become the central motivation for my writing this book.

Thanks also goes to Aggie for constantly badgering me to share my thoughts so more people could benefit as others already have. For her constant devotion to our family and her unbending support in my children's development and achievements, never wavering no matter what the

ACKNOWLEDGMENTS

circumstances. I love her as a sister, and my children love her as a mother.

To my grandchildren, Marissa, Darin, Amanda, Matthew, Taylor, Nikki, and Jake and to all the children of the world who will be our future leaders and who can make a difference, I humbly offer you this book.

To Phyllis, who through the years has listened to and watched the things I have achieved and inspired my writing, I give my deepest thanks. Without her gift of a traveling note pad, this book might never have started. She is like a sister to my daughters and like a daughter to me. Thank you, Phyllis, for your unending support.

Thanks to my childhood friend Jerry Dalven who is solely responsible for my choosing the field of architecture and for my seeking a college education. Without his guidance and faith, I might have had a much different life.

Thanks to all those people who have written to express their sincere gratitude for my help and who have encouraged me to put my thoughts in writing. I have saved every one of your letters.

One might not believe that angels exist, but for me, they do. For me, they exist not only in the spiritual world but also in the real world. My life has been filled with many people appearing as angels. They come in my darkest moments and guide me to the light. Ivan Goldfarb is one such angel. We shared a common experience from kindergarten to high school. We were always friendly then, but never best friends. Afterward, we went our separate ways. Ivan and I did not meet again until the both of us were in the sixth decade of our lives. The first time was a walk fifty years later on the boardwalk of our youth in Long Beach, New York. We talked for a while and there was an immediate connection. The timing could not have been more fortuitous. I was in the middle of the struggle to write this book when this angel descended into my life. Ivan Goldfarb—author, teacher, and friend—was to become my savior and another angel to lead me through the darkness.

To Ivan, without you, there would be no book, no testament to failure and triumph, no acknowledgment of the many good people in my life, and no record of the philosophy that has served me so well.

Lastly, my thanks to all the people in the world, people I have never met, who through their perseverance, openness to change, and an unbending belief in brainpower have accomplished the impossible. For example, there is the story of the young girl on the television program 20/20 who glowed with good health until she began suffering severe epileptic seizures. Her seizures grew into the hundreds during the course of a day. After exhaustive medical research by her parents, a decision was made to allow one-half of her brain to be removed surgically, the half responsible for the seizures. After the surgery, the girl's parents faced a potentially catastrophic future for their child. They searched for help so their daughter would not have to spend her life disabled psychologically and physically by the results of her operation. While they searched, their daughter languished on the edge of doom. Finally, someone suggested to the parents that the best results might come from an attitude change, a change that would lead to a more positive way of thinking for their child. Following that advice led to an amazing turnaround.

ACKNOWLEDGMENTS

Arduous years of therapy followed, but the young woman now walks and dances by herself. She is almost fully functional physically and an "A" student in school.

With positive brainpower, a young woman was able to accomplish what was virtually impossible. As time went on, professionals involved in her case discovered that through the girl's intense faith and commitment to improvement, the remaining side of her brain was able to assume many of the functions of the missing half.

This is a perfect example of brainpower at work. While reading my book, always remember this story and how brainpower changed a life most people had written off.

Chelsea School Keynote Graduation Speech

Upon nearing completion of this book something incredible happened that I would like to share with you, my readers.

My friend and attorney Herb Balin was chatting with a business associate. He was informed that her husband was involved with a school for dyslexic children. Herb immediately told him about me and my book. Together they placed a call, and over the phone, I was introduced to Tony Messina, director of the Chelsea School for Dyslexic Children, located in Silver Springs, Maryland.

I was shocked and speechless as I listened to his introduction. At seventy years of age, living with dyslexia my whole life, I never knew such a school existed. As a child growing up, no one knew about this affliction. I was considered hopeless and left to fend for myself. Tony and I met for a four-hour lunch at which time I was invited to visit Chelsea. A few weeks later in February of 2006, I found myself sitting in Tony's office preparing for a tour of the grounds and a visit to observe classes in session.

CHELSEA SCHOOL KEYNOTE GRADUATION SPEECH

This tour was extremely enlightening. What I did not know was that during the morning assembly prior to my arrival, Tony announced to the students and the teachers that they were getting a guest who had written a book. He then elaborated a bit about its author.

After touring the grounds, we entered our first class. Being unaware of the morning introduction, I thought I would fade into the background and observe.

"Mr. Weinstein I presume?"

"Yes, sir," I replied in total surprise. "We have been looking forward to meeting you and would love to have you address the class and share some of your experiences."

For two days, I talked and observed and what I observed was from another side of the teaching world. The interaction between Tony Messina, his teaching staff, and his students was something very special. Their warmth and their admiration were evident from all of the students and teachers we came in contact with.

The one-on-one instruction displayed in the classrooms was something I never before experienced. These special education teachers were totally committed to helping each individual with his learning skills.

To know that a school like Chelsea exists was a wonderful and enlightening feeling. Schools like this can only continue to thrive through the efforts of people like Tony Messina and his devoted teaching staff.

I am in total awe of the Chelsea School, and I thank them for inviting me to be a keynote speaker at their graduation on June 12, 2006. A copy of that speech follows; however, you may visit my YouTube channel to see it live by either entering the following URL http://youtu.be/ByMlvOLEJrU into your web browser or by typing in "Allen Weinstein Chelsea School Graduation Speech."

Graduation Speech, June 2006:

Good afternoon, ladies, gentlemen, and graduates. My name is Allen Weinstein, I am dyslexic and learning disabled, and I am a self-made multi-millionaire!

I want to thank Tony Messina, the board of Governors and the graduating class of 2006, for giving to me the honor of speaking on this special occasion.

I commend the parents for recognizing their child's problems and having the interest and taking the time to seek out such a school as Chelsea. During my visit in February, I had the opportunity of observing Mr. Messina, and his teaching staff. I give my personal thanks for the caring, the sincerity, and the dedication they exude while interacting with, and teaching their students—your children.

I congratulate the graduates on this auspicious day. Today you have reached a goal that was only obtainable through your will, your desire and a strong belief in yourself to achieve.

There must have been a time when some of you, your loved ones and your friends thought this day was unattainable, an impossible mission. However, we know better, we know nothing is impossible, nothing is unattainable; we know the future is only behind us, when we stop believing and dreaming of our goals.

CHELSEA SCHOOL KEYNOTE GRADUATION SPEECH

I am 70 years old and unfortunately, when I was in school no one knew of these problems so consequently I was labeled stupid, when asked how many Apple's I can purchase with a quarter if each Apple was a nickel I had no clue. I could not read until I was 13. Once I received a 30 on an exam and there were comments sent home to my parents that I had not studied. When I confronted the teacher about these comments his response to me was, "I should have known better in order for you to have received a 30 you had to have studied." This is just as small sample of what I had to endure during my school days from my teachers and at age appropriate, I was graduated. The school would not give me college applications and the staff and students labeled me the least likely to succeed.

However; there was one person who always believed in me, there was one person who would never listen to negative thoughts; one person who would never give up on me—just one—that person was me! Although it took me seven years, today I hold a degree in architecture from the University of Kansas, how can one who cannot figure out how the Apple's can be purchased for a quarter or score a 30 on an exam attain such a goal? Because of my conviction, and because the goals I set for myself, and because of my ability to imagine, along with my positive self-image failure was not an option.

There were many roadblocks, dead ends, bumps in the roads, hurdles and any other synonym you can think of. I started at Tulane University, and after three years was asked to leave. I went home on worked for an architect while attending night school. Later I was accepted to the

University of Kansas where I began to practice alternative methods to augment my learning disabilities.

So, as for the kid who was least likely to succeed I am one of the most successful graduates from my high school. Once again the obstacles were present every day. The struggle was constant and the challenges never ended.

The book I wrote which I will give to each of you graduates starts in 1975 on a Sunday evening I went to sleep with two million dollars in the bank and a company doing 75 million dollars of construction and 175,000 dollar income, in 1975 that was a lot of money. Monday morning I awoke BROKE overnight my entire company collapsed. How does this happen? That is for you to read in my book however; what I can tell you is for eight years I struggled to get back what I lost. During those eight years I never gave up, never allowed negative thoughts to control my future, I just kept a clear and decisive attitude always striving to reach the goals I had set for myself and because of my constant belief in myself today I am a self-made multimillionaire owning one of the most successful real estate companies on Long Island and I sit on the Board of directors of many other companies that I have invested in. Failure was never an option.

No one knows us as well as we know ourselves. We are a result of who we think we are. If we think we are incapable of achievement, if we think we cannot reach our goals if we think negative thoughts, then we will think ourselves into failure. However, if we think positive thoughts and train our minds to imagine our dreams, to set goals and to achieve our destinations, successes then is only a matter of time. Remember when you change the way you look at things the things you look at will change. To overcome my disabilities I used alternative methods I realized that the ability to achieve was limited only by your ability to imagine I found imagery or cyber vision, as it is called in sports, was one of the keys to my success.

We are unaware of it but we use imagery every day of our lives. Because we are unaware of it we do not focus on it or take advantage of its principles.

If I were to give a golf ball, a golf club, and a tee, to someone in a country having no communication with the outside civilization as we do, they would have no clue what to do with this equipment. If on the other hand I gave this same equipment to anyone in this room who has never played the game of golf they would know the principles of what to do. Why? Imagery.

They have seen it done so there for their mind knows what to do. The more we work on this image the clearer it gets and the clearer it gets the better we'd perform Nothing happens without an image, from the safety pin to the computer everything was an image in someone's mind and the images we can see in our minds become our goals and determine our destinations without it nothing can be accomplished.

This morning we all woke with one image, one goal, and destination, the image was that of seeing yourself your child's your relative or your friend receive their diploma. The goal and destination where to arrive here on time, no matter how long it took no matter the means of transportation you chose, coming from many different directions you all made it here in time. For those of you who may have hit a roadblock or traffic jam or a last-minute change in your transportation plans regardless you still made it. Those roadblocks did not discourage you, never once did you consider quitting and returning home, you just found another way around until you were back on your way to this theater. Why? Because, the image, the goal, and the destination were so a fixed in your mind that to fail was not an option.

Because of our disabilities we suffer from the overdose of negativity, consequently it is imperative that along this trip of life we continue to affirm our position, our thoughts, our images must always show that our goals are already attained, that we are enjoying a beautiful and successful life. Never waver from those images and they will become a reality, the mind is a powerful ally and it will never disappoint you.

The most sophisticated piece of equipment ever produced by man is the computer. The amount of information available to us is so voluminous and so diverse it has no equal, yet all the information that comes out of this complex piece of equipment was "programmed by many different human brains. If we find the information we are reading to be objectionable or just plain incorrect we use the same brain to program the information in so the information out changes. Folks make no mistakes about it we are all walking computers from birth to death, we are all programmed by many human brains. At inception both the human brain and the computer are void of knowledge. We are not born with knowledge we are taught it, we are not born with prejudice we are taught it, and we are not born ingrained with negativity it is fed to us by others. So if you're not pleased with the information fed to you through the years and if you do not like your self-image use your power of imagery to reprogram yourself to new life.

Ladies and gentlemen, a day like today is only made possible by a school like Chelsea. The future of your children and other children with dyslexia depend on the growth and success of this institution. You could not have a more motivated leader than Tony Messina or more dedicated teaching staff and board of governors. However, that is not always enough. This school needs your continued support in whatever form that is available. It is also imperative to have a strong and active alumni. I would like once again to congratulate the class of 2006, and remind them that tomorrow you are all alumni and to give back what you have received is a deed that is always rewarded, the sharing of experiences is what gives the experiences value, and that is why I am here to day.

Always keep in mind I am living proof that dyslexia and learning disabilities are not synonymous with failure! Thank you and best of luck to you all.

Part One

Synopsis of My Life

Losing It

It was a Sunday night, not unlike many others in my life at the time. I had returned home from dinner at my country club with my family. I was forty years old and a multimillionaire. I had achieved an impossible dream. A dream that saw a dyslexic kid, a kid who few people saw potential in, rise from his handicaps to become a respected and important member of his profession and community. Indeed, life had been good to me. On the night of February 5, 1975, I went to bed with that knowledge and with the security of knowing I had enough cash in my bank account and a host of other equally valuable assets. The wealth I possessed was enough to allow me to retire for life. It was a comforting place to be. I was perched at the top of my personal mountain overlooking a world that was firmly in my grasp as I closed my eyes and drifted off to sleep. I had it all: two fine children, a comfortable home, a solid business, a country club life, a ski house, and many friends. I didn't think it could get much better for me as I closed my eyes and drifted off to sleep. Then, the morning came.

I awakened to my usual routine. I took a quick shower, dressed, and listened to the news on the radio as I had breakfast. It all seemed very typical until I heard the radio

LOSING IT

announcer describe a major story that was unfolding on Long Island. A story that involved a bank failure. The bank was the Franklin National Bank, the twentieth largest in the United States and the largest bank on Long Island at that time. I knew Franklin well. It was a powerhouse with over five billion dollars in assets and more than one hundred branches from Floral Park to Montauk. Franklin was also my bank. If the story held up and Franklin was in the tank, I had a serious problem. Franklin held my money. More than that, it held notes on several major projects of mine that were backed by my savings, my assets, and my personal signature. I rushed from room to room turning on all the television sets in the house. Newscaster after newscaster continued the radio story. I realized that my world of yesterday had vanished. My immediate reaction on hearing the news of Franklin's shut doors was shock and disbelief. I thought it must be some other bank. I had just finished working with Franklin's bankers on Friday. Everything seemed normal then. But it was not so now. Franklin was defunct, and I was a man stripped of his life savings.

I was sitting in the living room, numbed by my ill fortune when my wife found me. I could barely bring myself to tell her about our reversal of fortune. She was white-faced and silent after I explained what happened. Neither of us knew quite what to say. Finally, I called Franklin in the hope I might find someone to speak to who could give me some information beyond my worst nightmare. But my calls were fruitless. No one was there to answer. However, within a few days, I had

1. *"The similarity between success and failure is one's state of mind."*

the answers to my questions. I owed the Federal Deposit Insurance Corporation and my contractors $13,800,000.00

The history of Franklin National Bank is instructive. Originally, it was the brainchild of its founder, Arthur Ross. Ross controlled the bank during a period of time when Long Island exploded with population and housing growth. Franklin provided loans for the hordes of builders who were trying to meet the housing needs of a rapidly swelling population. Its position was enhanced by the fact that New York City banks were prohibited at that time from having branches on Long Island. These two forces combined to give Franklin growth beyond Ross's wildest dreams. Thus, Franklin Bank became the central player in the building boom of Long Island during the 1950s and 1960s, and it was soon a billion-dollar bank.

When city banks finally were allowed to do business on the island, Franklin's days as the preeminent bank of Long Island were over. This development and Ross's questionable business practices led to Franklin becoming vulnerable. As Franklin's troubles grew, it came to the attention of an Italian investor, Michele Sindona. In the late sixties, Sindona seized the moment. He decided to invest in Franklin and for $40 million dollars bought approximately 20% of the parent holding company. This investment was part of a much larger strategy by Sindona of which one element was to reap profits by using his European banks as a foreign exchange machine with Franklin. No one was paying too much attention to that or Sindona's business background. He had money, and he had the wherewithal to change things at Franklin. By the year 1972, Sindona became president of the bank His plans for Franklin were put in motion, and they became an integral element in all of Franklin's problems. Central among these problems was Franklin's domestic performance. It was being hampered by a huge number of unprofitable loans. By 1974, Franklin's deficit had become astronomical, its indebtedness profound, and its liquidity virtually nonexistent. In hindsight, there was no effective supervision of Franklin by our government. Therefore, builders were destined to failure because Franklin could not continue to fund work to the completion of a construction job. As federal supervisors became aware of Franklin's troubles, they sought a solution that would be least damaging. Finally, they found an ally to assume control of Franklin in the European-American bank, a group of powerful European banks. European-American assumed control of Franklin's branches, deposits, and assets all of which were worth over three billion dollars. In essence, the bank consortium walked away with Franklin's assets, and its debtors had to fend for themselves. Those in government to whom Franklin was accountable had little regard for those of us who were left hanging by the bank's failure. Franklin's loans, loans to people like me, were placed under the jurisdiction of the Federal Deposit Insurance Corporation and New York State regulators. The goal of these agencies was simple: reclaim the billions of dollars still outstanding and disregard the fact that such an action could bankrupt many Long Island builders. In fact, there were literally hundreds of builders who became victims of this circumstance. I was one of those hundreds who became a part of the government's equation for clearing up the debacle of Franklin's failure.

Prior to this crisis, Franklin was the primary bank I used for most of my real estate projects. At that time, my prosperity was such that I entertained thoughts of retiring and entering the teaching profession to teach architecture. My ruminations about retiring reached the point where I went on a three-week vacation to review my options. While on vacation, I came to the conclusion that teaching might not be challenging enough for me and would not provide the kind of action and dynamics that I had become accustomed to in my business life. Then, I received a phone call from one of my partners who informed me that Franklin Bank would like to become a player in our real estate business but only if I was personally involved. It wasn't very long before I booked a flight home from my vacation wonderland. On the flight back, I thought about Franklin's interest in our business and considered Franklin's offer. At that time, banks were not allowed to be partners in businesses such as mine. As an important customer of Franklin, I would typically borrow money at 1% over the prime rate. However, under my new arrangement, I would borrow at 4.5% over prime and the difference between the 1% and the 4.5% is how Franklin would earn its portion of the profits. My advantage in working with the bank at these rates was the security in knowing I was backed to the hilt financially and able to tackle projects I might not otherwise obtain 100% financing for. In all other projects, any builder, whether it was I or someone else, had to put up 30% of the total cost of his projects. Therefore, my deal with Franklin made me the envy of every builder on Long Island who knew about it.

2. *"The worst day of your life is a welcome substitute for your last day."*

Ultimately, we were able to work a deal with Franklin for the financing of several major real estate ventures. The projects ranged from Long Island to Georgia. These ventures were the costliest I had been involved with since I began working with Franklin. The terms followed the pattern I expected except this time Franklin wanted my signature as well as other collateral. I was to provide this collateral through the personal savings I had deposited at Franklin and other equally valuable personal assets. Their position was understandable. After all, they would be putting up all the money, and in case of some unforeseen circumstance, they had no wish to be left with half-completed projects. Since I was as aware as Franklin that they could not legally be my partner, no part of our agreement could be put into writing. Therefore, the paperwork between us only reflected our loan agreement. I did not balk at these conditions. I had no reason to think anything was awry with Franklin. After all, this was a major bank, a powerful bank with great resources and a good public reputation. They also were the most prominent bank for builders on Long Island at that time, and I had worked with them often. My main contact at the bank, a loan officer, was a man who had proven helpful and trustworthy in obtaining financing for my ventures on many other occasions. I had nothing more than those positive perceptions to go on, so I approved the arrangement and signed the loan documents. I would live to regret that action. With our newly found financial resources, we started building a condominium complex called Artist Lake on eastern Long Island. Artist Lake was comprised of five hundred units in all and abutted a small lake from which the project derived its name. While in the process of building Artist Lake, I also started construction in Plainview, Long Island's Nassau County. That property, called the Villas, would hold approximately 130 condominium units. Additionally, we started to develop the Henry Ford Plantation in Savannah, Georgia. The plan was to build a golf course to host the Lady's PGA tournament. We were going to use the Ford home as the centerpiece of the project. Housing would be developed along the golf course and Ogeechee River. Any potential danger to the bank in these dealings had been eliminated by its arrangement with me. However, if Franklin had been my legitimate partner and not hiding behind the disguise of a building loan, when something went wrong, they would have had to continue funding until a job was completed or risk losing the partnership money. Since this was not the case, Franklin was in the catbird seat.

I had partners to help move all this work forward to completion. Each of my two partners handled a different aspect of the business. My role was primarily to make the deals that would allow our group to build properties on the land we acquired. My partners managed the actual construction and marketing of these deals. It proved to be a very good working arrangement.

My pact with Franklin to pay 4% over prime for their money led to a similar kind of arrangement with my contractors, only I was playing the role of banker. The contractors we dealt with would take notes from us at 1% over the prime rate. These usually were for thirty, sixty, or ninety days. Then the contractor's banks would lend them

3. *"To achieve in life, one must know his goal."*

money against the notes. Ninety days later, I would receive Franklin's money pay their notes off, and I would typically save 3 or 4% on interest for the time period. While this might seem to be piddling, when you are dealing in millions, the money I realized was no small amount.

    Needless to say, I was very pleased with the arrangement. Moreover, the contractors trusted the deal. They trusted me, and this led to a good working association. Projects were on schedule and the necessary money to drive each project to completion was there. Then Black Sunday came. However, Black Sunday was not the end of my problems with banks. There was another unexpected wrinkle to my financial situation. While Franklin National Bank was the provider of my building loans, I worked with another local bank, Bayside Federal Savings and Loan, to provide the mortgages to purchasers of my units. I would receive my money from Bayside and that money would be used to repay Franklin and the contractors. The remaining monies would be mine. Had everything gone along normally, this process would have given Franklin its money plus any interest, the contractors their piece of the pie, and my group its profits. Once Bayside discovered that Franklin National Bank was defunct, I was called in to meet with them. The meeting was within a week of Franklin's nosedive and would be the first of many meetings with bank and government officials. The flavor of this one was typical of most of my encounters. The president of the bank and one of his loan officers met with me at their headquarters in Queens, New York. The room we met in was generic bank—all browns and grays. I came to the meeting with one of my partners. We took seats in two wooden chairs opposite the two bank officials. We brought no documents with us. We were more interested in what they wanted than anything else. They greeted us with expressionless faces. We waited, curious about what they might have to say. The president spoke first.

"You're in a bad place, Allen, but I think we can help you and help ourselves."

"What is it you want to do?" I asked. My mind raced with the possibilities.

"If you can persuade your contractors to finish their work without further payment on their work in place until completion of the project, we'll pay them on a current basis. That way, you get what you want and we get what we want. The contractors get their monies and we take Franklin out of the picture completely. Do you think you might be able to swing something like that?"

At this point, the loan officer chimed in, "Yeah. Franklin would simply not be a part of any of this. You just have to bring in the contractors one by one to us. We need to be certain they accept our terms." His lips pulled back in what was supposed to be a smile. I saw his fingers tapping the tabletop. Waiting. For me, the suggestion was a ray of light in a black sky. It was a way to climb out of disaster and a way to restore my solvency and my life. Consequently, I said, "Yes."

I agreed to Bayside's proposal and made arrangements to bring in my contractors individually to meet with Bayside officials and me. One by one, each contractor agreed to continue work without any payment on work already in place, and each in turn was assured he would be paid by the bank for all future work and, at the end of the project, all past work. I was both overwhelmed by their response and humbled by it. They had other choices, but these were honorable men whom I had worked with before, and they knew me and they knew my word was good. In a strange way, their response was a validation of my business ethics and my personal standard of conduct.

The projects moved toward completion. I breathed a sigh of relief at the fact that despite all my problems, I was still in business and functioning. Months later, when it came time for the first of my contractors to be paid, my concrete supplier went to Bayside for payment as per his agreement. I barely noticed the timing. That is, until I received a call from him.

"Hey Allen. Fred here."

"What's up, Fred?"

"Allen, Bayside isn't paying."

"What do you mean?"

"You know that agreement we had?"

"Yeah."

"Well, forget about it, Bayside's changed its mind."

"Changed its mind?"

Yeah. Like in not paying. Bastards told me to go home. The deal is off."

"Son of a bitch! Fred, I gotta call the bastards. I'll get back to you."

"OK, Al."

I called the bank immediately. I asked for the president but got the loan officer instead.

"Hi, Al."

"Don't give me that 'Hi, Al' crap. Fred says you are not paying him."

"We're not. We changed our position."

"What? Just like that. You make a deal and then back out of it."

"It's a business decision. We always reserve the right to make business decisions."

"Yeah, well don't think I am going to let you off the hook without a major fight."

"I'm sorry, Al."

"Save it for your next rotten deal. I don't need you or your bank."

I hung up the phone, raging with fury and overwhelmed by this new turn of events. I tried to assess my situation and determine my options, but the shock of Bayside's betrayal weighed heavily on me and clouded my thinking. Perhaps, I reasoned, clarity would be restored in a calmer atmosphere. I had already made arrangements to go upstate for a few days of skiing and entertaining with a lawyer friend, Herb Balin. So I climbed into my car that Friday afternoon and made my run to Hunter Mountain, New York, where I had maintained a ski house for the previous five winters. The house was a three-hour drive up north of Long Island. I hardly noticed.

When I finally arrived, Herb Balin was already there. Herb was a prominent real estate attorney on Long Island and someone who had been friendly with me for some time. Business had never been part of our relationship. We were just good friends.

4. *"Appreciate what we have rather than agonize over what we do not have."*

LOSING IT

Over the weekend, he noticed that I was not my usual self and seemed preoccupied with other matters. Finally, one evening after dinner, he asked me to join him in the den. I sat down in an easy chair opposite him.

"What's the problem, Al? You don't seem to be yourself this weekend. What's going on? "Is everything ok at home or is it the business that's bothering you?"

"Well…you're right, Herb. You know the business with Franklin has been a nightmare for me."

"Yes, I know."

"I made a deal with Bayside. You might not know that. They agreed to pay my contractors at the end of the job. I had to bring in each one for verification by them. All of them agreed to finish the job and the loan officer promised to pay them in full after completion of their jobs. They all agreed. Well, Fred, my concrete guy went to get his money. Guess what? He was sent packing and told the deal was off. Fred called me. All pissed off. What could I say? What can I do? It's a nightmare. The bank pulled the rug right out from under me."

Herb studied me a moment. Then, he said, "You know, Allen, I love you like a brother, but you are not telling me the entire story. No bank can do what you say Bayside did. They just can't do that. There's something missing."

"Herb," I replied, "there's nothing missing. I've told you everything."

Well, OK, Al, if you say so. But it doesn't make any sense to me at all."

We sat around and talked some more and then went to bed. The next day we both returned to Long Island. On Monday, Herb called me at my office.

"It's me, Herb. Al, guess what?"

"What?"

"I've been hired by all the contractors to sue you and the bank for breach of contract."

"Jesus. That is nuts."

"What I wanted to tell you is that everything you told me is 100% true. But please understand, Al, the suit against you is not personal. It's just that the guys have to protect themselves. They are out on a limb just like you are. We really want to go after the bank, not you. The bank lied and played them for suckers."

"I understand. It's fine, Herb."

Soon afterward, I learned that Bayside had taken steps through the New York State attorney general's office to remove me from the project. They argued I could not complete the construction, and they were entitled to protect their investment also. In addition, Bayside contacted each homeowner living on the job site and explained if I was not removed as the builder, the remainder of the homes would not be completed. The homeowners would be living in Uglyville. Therefore, Bayside wanted New York's attorney general to remove me from any involvement with the condominiums.

Actually, the government had a responsibility to act on Bayside's request. It was operating under the mandate to protect the homeowner and not the builder in any building endeavor. If that meant introducing a solvent builder and discarding an insolvent one, then so be it. Thus, Bayside, the homeowners, and the attorney general were aligned against me. I was the bad guy. This was the backdrop to my first meeting in the New York City offices of the attorney general.

They were all there: the homeowner representatives, the Bayside officials, and the attorney general's people. The lead lawyer for the attorney general, Lefkowitz, spoke first. He was right to the point.

"Mr. Weinstein, as you know, the Artist Lake job has been halted, and we think it is in your best interest to sign over the deed to Bayside. We've reviewed their request, and it is clear to us that the homeowners would be better served if you were out of the loop so Bayside can finish the job with a different builder. Your good standing and reputation have been damaged by the Franklin mess. It's as simple as that."

"Really? It's not that simple for me. I've done nothing wrong, yet I have become a victim, and I am still being victimized by you and by Bayside. Now, I am a stubborn guy, and when I think I am right, I don't cave in very easily and I am not caving in now to you. I'll fight Bayside and you in court if necessary to vindicate myself and to save my business. What you are asking for is crap as far as I am concerned."

"Well, I'm not sure that's a good decision. Giving up the job would be."

"Yeah, in your opinion and the opinion of everyone else here." I waved my hand at the other parties seated at the table. "Yes. That is our opinion. I think I speak for everyone." He paused a moment and played his trump card. "By the way, I guess we will have to see your books then. Is there a time when we might do that?"

"You would be better served looking into the business practices of the bank instead of trying to give me the short

---

5. *"There are many people who are wealthier than I, but few richer."*

end of the stick. It seems to me that the bank is operating illegally. I'm not."

"That is not your call."

"You are not seeing my books. Maybe I might reconsider if you look into the bank's practices first and how they lied to and cheated the contractors and me. Maybe then. But no way will you look at me first. No way. Don't look at me first. Look at the bank first. You've got it backward. They are the crooks and they are sitting right there next to you."

I pointed my index finger at the Bayside officials for emphasis and then I sat back in my chair. The room was silent. It appeared no one could believe I had the temerity to say what I did to the attorney general's representatives.

"I know you are under a lot of pressure, Mr. Weinstein. We'd like you to think over our request and we'll do the same thing."

"There is nothing for me to think about. You don't get near my books until you look at theirs. I said it before, the very people in this room representing the bank are liars and crooks as far as I am concerned. This meeting is over." I rose from my seat and left the room followed by my accountants and lawyers.

6. *(As quoted by many)* *"It is not how often you fall that counts; it is how often you rise."*

Notes

The FDIC

The FDIC wanted their share of the 13.8 million dollars they thought I was accountable for. They made no bones about it either. I was called in to meet with them in New York City. The building our meeting was held in was located on the west side of Manhattan not too far from Penn Station. It was a drab place and so was the room I entered for the meeting. It was apparent to me the FDIC had bankers' ideas about frills and nonessentials. I went to the meeting without an attorney. I wasn't intimidated by them, and I was angry more than anything else. If the FDIC thought they could intimidate me, they had the wrong man. If they thought they could get some kind of confession and unreserved cooperation, they had the wrong guy. My view was that Franklin had an obligation to live up to its arrangement with me. If you agree to loan someone money to do a job, then you agree to do that until the job is completed. As far as I was concerned, the governmental agency responsible for some of Franklin's policies and Michele Sindona's stewardship was trying to wiggle out of the situation by laying blame on people like me. I wasn't going to be anyone's patsy. As I saw it, the government should have been helping me and not trying to bury me. When I took my seat, I was struck by the sameness of these

THE FDIC

people, the people I dealt with from Franklin, Bayside, and now the FDIC. They were virtually interchangeable, as bland and unremarkable as a kitchen pot. We introduced ourselves and shook hands.

Three officials represented the FDIC. I took them all to be lawyers. The lead person was a tall, thin, and dour man. He spoke first.

"Allen, you understand that our job is to recover our part of the 13.8 million dollars you owe as a result to your dealings with Franklin National Bank."

"I understand that I have obligations in that regard, but do you understand your obligations?"

"What do you mean?" He seemed surprised by my response.

"I mean that had you and the other regulators done their jobs properly, we wouldn't be having this conversation, I and many other builders wouldn't be bankrupt, and Franklin wouldn't be shut down. That is what I mean."

"We do our job, Allen. That's why we are here today. To make certain that people who owe money, pay their debts."

"As far as I am concerned, you guys are the guilty ones. I did nothing wrong. I'm an honest businessman who has been hurt as much as anyone by the bank's practices and your failures to regulate it. Now, I am expected to pay for everyone else's mistakes."

"We don't see it that way, Allen."

"It's not your business to be objective about this stuff. You're just looking for fall guys to pay for other people's

---

7. *"You are what you believe. You can be what you imagine."*

failures, and I am a convenient pigeon. How do you let a banker from another country come into the states, take over one of the largest banks in the United States, and sit by until it is run into the ground? What is your responsibility? What is your accountability?"

"We are not the ones who owe the money. You do."

"You didn't answer my questions. You can't. Franklin is busted because of its policies and the failure of your oversight. The right thing for you guys to do would be to fund my job to completion and then everyone wins. Not this."

"Well, you don't have an agreement for continued funding, do you?"

"Look if a person has a building loan, and the building is not finished, don't you think the lender has an obligation to complete his commitment?"

"No, we don't have that obligation. We are not the lender. He is out of business."

"What is your obligation then? Just screwing me and other honest businessmen?" The meeting ended on that note.

Five years went by before the storm cleared. Five years of anxiety, frustration, anger, and uncertainty. I went to court virtually every day. I was out of business, in debt to the government, and just about everyone else who had been part of my professional life. I tried to eliminate expenses like my membership in the local country club. However, in an unprecedented decision by the club, I was given a three-year leave of absence. I tried to dismiss my housekeeper, Aggie, but she insisted on remaining and working for me without pay. She told me I could repay her at some future time. (She has been with me ever since.) I stopped paying rent on my ski house but the owner, cognizant of my misfortune, insisted I use it rent-free until better times came. I was stunned and humbled by the gestures of these good people. However, people who didn't know my true circumstances thought I was still prosperous since I still had my ski house and Aggie. I learned how easily appearances deceive.

My lawyer was my most important friend now. Working with him and putting food on the table for my family and paying the rent became the central issues in my life. It was a difficult time. I knew I had to return to the real estate business, but I hadn't quite figured out how. So I did just about anything within my expertise to earn money. I drew up home and building plans for a fee. I worked for other people.

I borrowed money when I had to. Somehow or other, I cobbled together enough cash to pay my bills. During these bad days, I never considered giving up my quest for justice or lost my determination to regain what I had lost. I never let the thought of failure enter my mind. I knew I had done nothing wrong. I knew I would ultimately prevail. I just knew. Not once during these terrible years did I consider bankruptcy although everyone around me said this was the best course of action for my business survival.

Needless to say, the stresses on my life were overwhelming. One of the most important ways I dealt with the daily grind was exercise. I began a program of workouts that has remained with me until this day. The mind-clearing benefits of rigorous physical activity became a staple of my life. I began with running and that soon morphed into weight training

---

8. *"It is not circumstance that shapes our minds, but our reaction to it."*

also. I loved the physical exercise and the feeling of well-being that went along with it. My workouts somehow gave me the ability to cope and to endure.

Another great support for me during these years was a friend, Julian Jarwitz. Julian was both a brilliant lawyer and an engaging personality. As an attorney, Julian had represented me in a variety of business dealings. He was retired when he first learned about my troubles. I had been good to him during our years of business together, and he never forgot. Thus, he came out of his retirement to help me. Julian took complete control of my legal affairs for almost six years. He never asked me for a penny in compensation.

His incredible generosity and strength and his unique talents were as much a part of my ultimate vindication and revival as anything else.

During the bad years, the attorney general began an investigation of Bayside and its practices. It turned out that Bayside's motivation in dealing with me centered on the fact that they had their own developer in mind for my unfinished work. Getting me out of the picture, therefore, was a part of their business and political strategy. The attorney general's office would be the tool used to remove me from the picture. It almost worked. When the attorney general threatened me with the weight of the law. The presumption was that I would cave in. This idea was based on the fact that many builders used their building loans not only for business but also for personal needs. Of course this was illegal. They assumed that about me. They were wrong. I never did anything like that, and when they threatened me, I stood fast. I knew I was clean. More than that I was outraged by the sleazy attempt to force me to surrender what I had created. They knew who I thought the real culprits were.

The attorney general finally decided to investigate Bayside's business activities in connection with the Franklin disaster as a result of my continual refusal to show my books and the constant pressure from frustrated and angry homeowners. Thus, it came as no surprise to me when Bayside was fined for its dealings in the matter nor was I shocked to learn that Bayside dismissed all the officials I dealt with during those terrible years. It was a vindication of sorts.

In addition to Julian Jarwitz, no one was more important to me in all of this than Herb Balin. Herb, as lawyer for the contractors, in effect was working for me. If he was successful in his lawsuit, it would have a direct and positive impact on my case. As it turned out, Herb did win his case, and Bayside had to pay the contractors who had been left hanging. For me, it meant Bayside had to pay the debts in relation to my dealings with the FDIC. So the FDIC settled with Bayside over my debt, and I was free from their clutches, but I still lost the two million dollars in cash that Franklin held. Herb and Julian saved the day for me, but I was still left with the fact that I had gone from riches to penury.

Although many people had suffered mightily with me during these years, we all managed to endure. And somehow, out of the wreckage of the Franklin National Bank failure, I found the will to start over and forge a new life for myself from the wreckage. Eventually, the people who had always

9. *"Success has a unique meaning for each of us."*

been my investors returned to me, and years after the onset of the Franklin debacle, I was able to reenter the real estate business. The painful lessons I learned from this period in my life remains with me to this very day.

10. *"Nothing is real. Everything is perception."*

Notes

Long Beach

I came from a place named Long Beach, Long Island, a narrow sand bar three miles long and maybe a half-mile wide at its thickest point. Henry Hudson, it is said, saw it first in 1609. Long Beach then and now was but one of the many barrier beaches that faced the Atlantic and protected the south shore of Long Island. At one time, it was a home to the Far Rockaway Indians until the white man came along and discovered its sandy shores and shallow bay as a fine place to fish. Later on at the end of the nineteenth century its development began. The Long Island Railroad had much to do with it. Its railroad line ran from Manhattan to Long Beach, just a short forty-five minutes. A group of wealthy investors acquired development rights to the area and for those who could afford it the glorious white beaches and pounding surf became a summer refuge from the heat of the city. The world's largest hotel, the Long Beach Hotel, was built on its sandy shore to house the well-heeled and elite. Long Beach remained a playground for the rich until one William Reynolds came along in 1907. Observing the attractiveness of the place for the wealthy, Reynolds, a state senator who helped develop Coney Island, decided further development of Long Beach could be another profitable business venture.

Construction began. Elephants from the Ringling Brothers circus were used to help build the three-mile boardwalk and to lay the huge boulders for jetties. The jetties, which stretched out like rocky fingers into the Atlantic, were used to control littoral drift and keep the beaches stabilized. The bay also received attention. A channel between Long Beach and the mainland was dredged so that large boats could ply the bay and drop their passengers off on the tiny island. A new hotel was built after the Long Beach Hotel burned down. The new three-hundred-room structure, the Nassau Hotel, was to be the focal point of the emerging community. The movers and shakers of the world arrived and soon other hotels were built and then homes. (Today the old Nassau Hotel is known as the Ocean Club Condominium.)

Reynolds set the rules in his paradise. Long Beach was to be a certain way for certain people. Not everyone was welcome. The Jews, Italians, Irish, and other ethnic and racial groups who would later populate the city were no more welcome than the Native Americans who once lived there. Housing also had to fit Reynolds's plan. A Spanish motif was chosen for Long Beach's homes: red tile roofs and white stucco exteriors. Giant, palatial homes were built for the wealthy. Since land was scarce, the homes were almost as large as the plots they were erected on. The city hall and the railroad station echoed this beautiful architecture as well as the red brick streets for the well shod to walk on. The streets were divided by broad grassy malls that gave a park-like atmosphere to the town. A splendid main street, the eponymous Park Avenue, was constructed and paved with cobblestones. All of this helped give the place a unique flavor. Long Beach thrived.

The affluent came, and they lived the good life there. During Prohibition, the mob ran booze through the town, largely because Long Beach was a convenient place to offload liquor and then transport it to the mainland. None of this damaged the reputation of Long Beach as a place where fun or a drink could be found if a person had the money. Then, the Great Depression struck, and Long Beach began a new chapter in its existence.

I was born during the Great Depression. The year was 1935. I was the youngest of three sons. Social Security was created that same year and Franklin Roosevelt was president. I entered a world undergoing massive change and on the cusp of the greatest war the world had ever known. I was born in the city of Long Beach and in one way or another would remain there in body or spirit for the next six decades. In 1935, Long Beach was no longer Reynold's Long Beach. Long Beach had become a blue-collar town as well as a resort for the rich. People liked it not only for its splendid beaches and languid summers but because it was a safe place to raise children. Doors were left unlocked. Crime was something on the mainland or in the movies but not in Long Beach. Long Beach was not such a place. People knew one another too well. There were no secrets. If a person had a new job, people knew. If a person was a communist, people knew. If a family needed food on the table, people knew. If someone committed a crime, people knew. Long Beach was that kind of place where I drew my first breaths on earth.

My parents were naturalized American citizens. My mother came from England, and my father from Russia. My parents did not often talk about their roots. Like many

Jewish immigrants, they shrouded Europe and their past in a dark cloud. Being American to these new immigrants meant letting go of a painful history and becoming assimilated into American culture. My parents fit this profile perfectly. If I had relatives in England or Russia, I never knew about them.

Both my parents were in the hat business. My father manufactured a line of inexpensive women's hats from a rented building in New York City. The hats were manufactured by countless women at endless sewing machines. Money came in, but my father never became wealthy from his life's work, but he provided well enough for our family.

My father was a hardworking man. A man who, when he wasn't at work, liked to smoke cigars and fish. He would fish almost every weekend he could. At first it was from a rowboat, but later on it was from a powerboat. I rarely went fishing with him. My parents had less than an ideal marriage. As a result, I can't characterize my home life as happy. In a large part, I was raised by my nanny, Nellie. She was kind, gentle, and loving; and I always felt secure in her care. It is she who would read to me, play games with me, or take me for a walk into town.

As it turned out, my mother was more successful than my father in spite of the fact that she lived in an era when women had little opportunity. She was street smart, determined, and clever in business. A four-foot-eight-inch bundle of energy with a dynamic and forceful personality, she left no doubt about who was in charge. Her business was a lady's hat shop in Long Beach. It was located on Park Avenue in the Lafayette Building. Her store was on the second floor. It had a small show window on Park Avenue where she would display her newest designs. The shop featured my mother's creations exclusively, and she was widely known throughout Nassau County for her work. Her influence on me was significant in many ways, not the least of which was her creativity. I derived from her the ability to visualize my ideas in complete detail without ever drawing them. In addition I acquired her talent for taking disparate materials, even what some might call junk, and creating something from them that attracted the attention of people.

My mother was a friendly and open person as well as being generous and tolerant. She never divided people by race or by wealth. She liked anyone who was a good person, but if you were someone who was dishonest or mean-spirited, you were treated accordingly. She was "Kitty" to just about everyone who knew her, and someone who, despite her physical size, had an aura about her the size of Mount Rushmore. I know my mother passed on all these qualities to me. She also gave me her indomitable spirit and will to succeed. To this day, people stop me and reminisce with joy and wonder about how she made their wedding and holiday hats. Some have still kept them along with the specially designed hatboxes for them. Many of these people have given these artifacts of my mother's work to me. I cherish them as much as anything I have in life. My brothers were another strong influence on my life. I idolized my brothers. Perhaps, that was due to our age difference. Joe was nine years older than I, and Warren was seven years older. But we had our fun and games as kids. Not the least of which was wrestling. Since they both were on the wrestling team, they liked to practice with one another and with me. That was a distinct disadvantage to me given their maturity in relation to mine. However, we never fought in a strict sense of the word, as brothers often do. It was not that way with us.

Eventually, Warren joined the United States Air Force. His goal was to be a captain for American Airlines. He did just that with his life, and he is now happily retired and lives in Los Angeles. Joe and I were in business together for forty years and never had a fight. We moved about a bit in Long Beach and finally the family settled into a two-family white stucco house on West Market Street. West Market Street was located in the center of town and a short walk from just about every important place—the city hall, the train station, the post office, the library, my elementary school—and Long Beach's stores were within minutes. Best of all, the beach was within five short blocks and the bay three blocks. All of this for $8,000.

Houses were jammed together in Long Beach. Space was at a premium even then. Single-family homes were the exception and not the rule. Some homes did have detached garages, but many did not. We had one even though our house was on a tiny plot of land that could barely hold a Victory Garden. In every way, our home was as ordinary as a housefly except for one distinguishing feature. We had one of the famous red tile roofs of the Reynold's era. The apartment we lived in was on the first floor of the house. We had three bedrooms, a bathroom, a living room, a dining room, and a kitchen. It was not spacious by today's standards, maybe 1,200 square feet of living space, but it was fairly typical of the housing space for many people living in Long Beach at that time. However, all that was lost on me. To me as a child, one of the most important attributes of my home was its front porch and stoop. It is there I would play stoopball with my friends. It was there we would sit talking about the war, movies, or the beach on countless summer nights. It was there we'd sit on the cement steps burning punk to ward off the mosquitoes and watch all the other people sitting outside for the evening in just the same way we were. For everyone, the front porch was a place of comfort in a world largely without room air conditioners. It seemed like life would always remain the same then: slow and easy, friendly and uncomplicated.

My other favorite place in our home was the basement. During World War II, we had to burn coal. Virtually every home had its heating plant changed to coal. To burn the coal, homes had to have coal bins built in their basements. Ours was an 8 × 10 walled area. After the war, the coal bin became my workshop and refuge. I had no electric tools, but I did manage to collect many hand tools from a variety of sources. Therefore, the drills, hammers, screwdrivers, planes, gouges, files, and clamps that I needed to build things were available to me. No one taught me how to use these tools. I taught myself by working with them, and I built furniture and about anything else that was of interest to me. One of my earliest projects was a bookcase followed by a desk. I also made radiator covers for the radiators in our house. After I finished a job, I would take the parts out through the 2 × 3 window that had been used as the entrance for the coal chute and reassemble them in the house.

11. *"Not all who have vision can see."*

LONG BEACH

My mother had two sisters and a brother. They were very close, almost inseparable. In fact, my mother bought our house with my Uncle Lou and Aunt May, who was my mother's sister. They lived in the upstairs apartment in our house in the summer. For the remainder of the year, they were in Brooklyn. My uncle and his wife were good people, and I was close to both of them and their children. For me, they were surrogate parents and treated me like one of their own.

Jack Irving was my mother's brother. He lived among the rich and famous on Hibiscus Island in Florida. I was in school in his most influential and powerful days. At that time, my uncle was resident of the American Guild of Variety Artists, the most dominant of all actors' unions.

Jack had no children and, consequently, was especially considerate and good to all his nieces and nephews. I loved my "Uncle Joe," as he was known in the family. He was always very generous to me and would intercede on my behalf in almost any kind of matter that required help.

I knew his sphere of influence was broad, but I did not ever take advantage of his position. Perhaps, this was because I was too young, naive, and inexperienced. He certainly could have ushered me into a career in show business, a career that others could only dream of. I just did not take advantage of what he could offer me. However, I did walk through the doors he opened for me to Broadway shows, Hollywood events, and big name performers.

For example, when I was at Tulane, Jerry Lewis and Dean Martin appeared in the Blue Room of the Roosevelt Hotel. I was at my frat house when I received a phone call. I was told by a frat house buddy that the call was from Jerry Lewis. I looked at the messenger of these tidings as if he was a lunatic, but I took the phone call, and indeed, it was Jerry Lewis. My shock was only exceeded by Jerry Lewis's generosity. He invited me and six of my friends to his show and treated me as if I was a member of his family. Me, a kid from Long Beach, Long Island, with no credentials in life and a learning disability. It was only one of many instances when my Uncle Joe's hand touched my life in ways I never expected. But I never played my ace in the hole.

I had a strong sense of family from these relationships and that has remained with me throughout my life. More than anything though, I was a child of the Second World War. It was everywhere around me. You couldn't live in Long Beach and not know about it or about patriotism. Sailors and marines were our neighbors now. However, the most dominant manifestation of the military was the naval base built at the east end of town. That was followed by the boardwalk, which became home to howitzers and machine guns pointed out to the Atlantic. Invasion fear ran high. The town buzzed with talk of the war. The general level of tension was raised when radar towers were built. These huge concrete structures whose antennae scanned the horizon for planes, submarines, and whatever else might be lurking beyond human sight were a daily reminder of a world in conflict. When the day gave way to night, everything in Long Beach was blacked out. My father and other fathers too old for the military walked the darkened streets as wardens, looking for potential danger but never finding it. Everyone waited for bombs to fall, but they never came.

LONG BEACH

We had parades in those days. Parades to celebrate our national holidays and our heroes. The entire town would turn out and honor all those who had served in World War I or World War II. We also had paper drives and drives for silver foil to help the war effort. I took part in those collections and anything else that a child of my age could participate in during those difficult war years.

In many homes a tiny flag in a window would signify a member of that household in the military. Some of those who went did not return. Their flags were draped in black. Everyone in town would know about these losses and mourn. That was the way it was in Long Beach. I was also a child of the nuclear age, radio days, and the birth of television. I matured in a world that saw mothers go to work and the traditional family dissolve. The idea of divorce began to take hold even in Long Beach and conventional values began to erode like the shoreline. An ethic was born: if you could get away with something, it was okay. I didn't reflect too much on those things while I was growing up. Going to the Laurel Theater to see a film for five cents or going to the beach was much more to my liking and the level of my insights.

The sea was always a large part of everyone's life in Long Beach. We were surrounded by salt water, with its smell always permeating the air. The ocean and the bay were always no more than minutes from my house. I could go down to the shoreline and dig clams and mussels out with no more effort than drinking a cup of coffee. Everyone fished in Long Beach. At first I fished off the dock at the end of Magnolia Boulevard. All that was needed was a bamboo pole, a float, a few snapper hooks, and bait. That's how kids fished for snappers, the immature version of the bluefish, in Long Beach. I would go to the old wooden dock and lean against the rails turned gray by the salt air. My friends and I would drop our lines and wait. In season, the wait was not very long. The fish were plentiful then and easy to catch. When we fished for flounder or fluke, the bait was Kellies and a rod, a reel, and a sinker. Whenever we caught a fish, it was always accompanied by a sense of wonder and accomplishment.

When I wasn't fishing or simply at the docks hanging around the boats in the summers, I was at the beach. The hot sun, the sea breeze, the roar of the surf, and the cries of children became the song of my life. As I grew older, wading into the ocean turned into swimming in the ocean. Then, it was body surfing, riding the waves into the shore. There were no surfboards or wet suits in Long Beach, just a neatly timed plunge into the face of a wave and, if it was caught correctly, a breathtaking ride into the beach.

Long Beach was a place of smells. You always smelled the salt air, and if you took a lungful deep enough, it would almost hurt. If it wasn't the salt air to be smelled, it was the stuffy, stale leathery air of Sabrett's hardware store. The smell of old wood, oiled machines, and cardboard boxes permeated every nook and cranny. But most of all, there was the smell of the pickle barrel in Leo's grocery store. Leo's was the place where people shopped before there were supermarkets. It was a small store on the first floor of the Parkway Court, a five-story apartment house on Park Avenue. It was a place I would go with my mother and later with my friends for the express purpose of fishing out a huge green sour pickle from Leo's magic barrel. There was more fun in that than the actual eating of the pickle. I also admired the fact that Leo hand-painted all his store signs. I was so impressed by his artistry that I would watch him for hours as he delicately painted his signs in beautiful scripts.

The beach was also the place where the city of Long Beach would bring orphans from the New York City orphanages for a day. If you lived in Long Beach, there was no way to miss their arrival. The entire town would turn out for it. A part of the beach would be set aside for the children and everything the beach and the boardwalk had to offer would be theirs for the day. They would come into the town in buses preceded by the screaming sirens of police department motorcycles. There was no way not to know that it was Orphan's Day, and no way not to know you were lucky not to be one of them.

Long Beach was a town of politics. It was one of two cities on Long Island. Unlike the vast majority of communities on Long island, both Long Beach and Glen Cove, the other city, had a government dominated by the Democratic Party. The Democratic Party in Long Beach was controlled by one man: the Democratic leader. In Long Beach, that was a man named Phil Kohut. He was the single most powerful political figure in town and all decisions about Long Beach, from who was hired to clean the beaches to real estate zoning, fell under his purview. Phil was "The Man." Whatever someone wanted done in town, Phil had to give approval. Early on in my life, I heard his name in my house and in the streets. The first time I actually met him I was thirteen years old. I was sent to see him by my mother. I wanted to work, and Phil was the means to acquiring a summer job. So I went to his office in the Grenada Towers looking for a job and uncertain what to expect. When I finally was ushered into his room, I saw Phil sitting behind a large mahogany desk in a brown leather chair. My immediate impression was of a tall, lean, blue-eyed, bald man. A huge cigar jutted from his mouth. His voice was gruff and authoritative when he spoke.

"So, you are Kitty Weinstein's kid?"

"Yes, sir."

"Where would you like to work?"

"The beach, Mr. Kohut."

"Well, you report to City Hall on Monday and take this note I'm writing with you. You'll work with the beachcombers."

"Thank you."

I took the note and I left. I was hired the next day.

Everyone seemed to have a connection to Phil Kohut in one way or another. If it wasn't a job, it was another kind of favor. Perhaps, it was helping with a parking ticket. It was that way with my mother. There was no free parking space in town and almost every day she would receive a ticket as she parked her car for work. At the end of the month, she would pay a visit to Phil, hand him the tickets, and that would be the end of it. So even as a child, I had an idea that the political process ran through people, people who did favors and received something in return for them. It was a lesson that was not lost in me. Phil Kohut and I would cross paths often in Long Beach and later on when I was in real estate and construction we would do business but that is another story. By the time I was a teenager, I was pretty much on my own. I had no rules and would go out at night with impunity. I felt there was nothing for me at home and no good reason to be there. Often I would be at a friend's house, but in the summer, I mostly went to the beach.

All the kids in town did. It was utterly safe and risk-free. I would meet my friends there after finishing whatever work I was doing for that summer. Often we would build a fire from the driftwood washed ashore. It would be one of many that were sprinkled along the beach from one end of town to the other. Sometimes we would cook potatoes by wrapping them in aluminum foil and burying them in the sand under the fire. Other times we would toast marshmallows or simply sit around and talk about our day, life, or girls. Girls mostly.

There was the boardwalk too. It was a home to me. In the winters after a snowstorm, we would slide down the ramps on our Flexible Flyers at breakneck speed. In warmer weather, we would build little wooden cars made from modified orange crates and place the crate on two-by-fours. Then we would attach skate wheels to the two-by-fours and off we would go.

It was glorious fun. Almost as glorious as jumping off the boardwalk onto the beach to avoid paying the entrance fee or going under the boardwalk and looking up through the cracks hoping for a glimpse of heaven under a girl's skirt. After the war, it seemed to me the entire town could be found on the boardwalk. People walking along stopping for an ice cream cone or sugar candy or playing games in the penny arcade. The sights, smells, and sounds were a symphony of life. To me it was an unending panorama. It was the world.

My street was also a world. It was a place of games. We played punch ball. We played mumblety-peg. We played stoopball. We played marbles. We flipped baseball cards.

We played stickball and basketball. If there was a game to be played, we played it.

One of my happiest times was my bar mitzvah. It was held at Temple Israel in town. It was special to me because I felt attention had been turned to me. For once I was not anonymous. Although I couldn't read Hebrew, I was able to memorize what I had to say. My memory was a blessing, and it served me well as I stood before the one hundred or so guests. I was confident and unafraid. More than that, I was at the center of things, and I liked the feeling. I was never excluded from any group in Long Beach. As I grew up, I floated from one clique to another. I was simply accepted. No muss. No fuss. It could have been otherwise, but it was not so.

Long Beach gave me a joy of life I have never lost. It gave me independence, and it gave me friends. It taught me the lessons of humility, trust, generosity, and tolerance. But most of all, Long Beach bestowed on me a spirituality that has been an integral part of my life and my success.

12. "Youth is wasted on youth unless we choose to embrace it."

Notes

We played stickball and basketball. If there was a game to be played, we played it.

One of my happiest times was my bar mitzvah. It was held at Temple Israel in town. It was special to me because I felt attention had been turned to me. For once I was not anonymous. Although I couldn't read Hebrew, I was able to memorize what I had to say. My memory was a blessing, and it served me well as I stood before the one hundred or so guests. I was confident and unafraid. More than that, I was at the center of things, and I liked the feeling. I was never excluded from any group in Long Beach. As I grew up, I floated from one clique to another. I was simply accepted. No muss. No fuss. It could have been otherwise, but it was not so.

Long Beach gave me a joy of life I have never lost. It gave me independence, and it gave me friends. It taught me the lessons of humility, trust, generosity, and tolerance. But most of all, Long Beach bestowed on me a spirituality that has been an integral part of my life and my success.

12. *"Youth is wasted on youth unless we choose to embrace it."*

Notes

School Days

I went to an elementary school within walking distance from my house. Of course, all schools were theoretically within walking distance in those days. There was no such thing as a school bus to get a child to school. Teachers were less skilled and trained than those of today and schools were far more rigid and limited in their approach to education. My school was one of three elementary schools in Long Beach. Its name was not very memorable: Central School. It was named so because it was located in the center of Long Beach. Central School was a three-story rectangular red brick building with a peaked roof. It was a large structure for Long Beach. The upper two floors housed the classrooms and the lower floor a gym and office space. The building always reminded me of a medieval fortress, huge and foreboding. But more than that, it was a place of mystery to me, a place of secrets.

It would remain that way for many decades until someone had a bright idea and turned the building into condominiums. The kindergarten classroom had an exterior entrance of its own. I remember walking up those concrete steps into a large room thick with a variety of toys and blackboards. A small playhouse was placed in its center. It was there the girls would play and pretend to be mothers while serving one another with tiny tea sets. There was also a seesaw and a blue-and-white wooden boat that could be rocked by those who sat in it. That was the good part of kindergarten. The difficult part was the teacher, Miss Kelley, a tiny but feisty woman who struck fear in just about everyone's heart. She was not a good introduction to teachers or to school. My initial response to Miss Kelley and school was to throw up every day before class for the first week, but soon I learned to play with the other children in kindergarten and some of the terror left me. As it turned out, the best part of kindergarten for me was that many of the children in the class would be my friends for life.

By the time I was in the first grade, I knew I had a problem. Letters and numbers were difficult for me. I found them perplexing and confusing. I struggled to understand what they meant and how they were used. I wasn't very successful. I just never understood phonics. Letters and words seemed jumbled together. I couldn't sound out anything. What I was trying to read could well have been Chinese. It was all the same to me. It didn't help my self-esteem to see all my peers progressing while I fell further and further behind. In fact, in all my years in school—any school—I never read a book cover to cover. I didn't know how to explain this handicap to anyone, least of all my parents. I didn't know how to talk about it to them or anyone else for that matter. My problems didn't become any better as time passed.

As each grade came and went, my difficulties in school multiplied. I tried ceaselessly to unlock the mystery of our language and the mystery of math, but to no avail. Everyone who knew me when I was in school also knew I was a poor student. My parents knew. My teachers knew. My friends knew. And of course, I knew. After each summer vacation, I dreaded going back to school.

I grew to hate Sundays because the next day was a Monday. Things being what they were then, I had no one to talk to about my curse. I suffered alone. In class, I was always fearful about being asked a question because I did not have an answer. I just couldn't read.

I wanted to be like my peers in school, but I could not nor did I ever find a method to cope. So I agonized and struggled academically. There seemed no way I could achieve respectability in school scholastically. Otherwise, school was fine. Other students liked me and I never had a sense of being ostracized or picked on. All of my teachers were indifferent until I reached the sixth grade. Then, I had Dr. Klein.

Dr. Klein was a kind and gentle man. No matter what kind of student you were, he accorded your respect. Somehow, he saw something worthy in me even though I always had the lowest score on his tests. To remedy the effect this was having on me, one day he gave me the answers to the next day's exam and let me take them home. I memorized the answers and received a hundred. This process went on for some time. I never told anyone. I would have my grade of 100 read aloud by Dr. Klein and everyone would look at me in amazement. I was no longer the class dunce. However, my success also made me want to achieve such results on my own, but I just couldn't and I didn't know why. It was very frustrating, and I was smart enough to know the next grade level and teacher would bring failure

---

13. *"When emotions control actions, the results are brainless."*

again. At that time there was not too much in place for a dyslexic and/or learning-disabled student in the Long Beach school system. There was one class that was designated for the unfortunates who were learning disabled or dyslexic. It was called the "Special Class." The Special Class was a hodgepodge of students from different grade levels. To be placed in that group meant being a virtual outcast and being labeled a "dummy" by one's peers. Placement in that group was not something either my parents or I could endure. Notwithstanding those reservations, I still was placed in this class for a semester. There were no expectations there, and nothing was done to help me with my disability. However, I did make a friend. His name was not one easily forgotten: Napoleon Bonaparte. Napoleon was one of the few black children in the school, and although I had no sense of race, I could not help but marvel at the coal black color of his skin. Napoleon had an outgoing personality and was fun for me to be with. We did many things together and were good for one another. Once, when he called my home and asked for me, my mother answered the phone and inquired who the caller was. When he announced "Napoleon Bonaparte," she placed the phone receiver in its cradle. When we talked about it, she later apologized, but it was then she realized my placement in the Special Class and raced off to the school the next day. I was soon out of the Special Class. I never returned. Napoleon was not as fortunate, but we remained good friends.

14. *"Weakness is a poison, which is a failure of the mind."*

Thus, elementary school by and large was a desperate time of life for me as I tried to survive in the classroom with my peers. Looming in the future was junior high school and high school. The transition to junior high school and high school was frightening in more ways than one. In Long Beach there was just one building to house all students from seventh to twelfth grade. When a student entered in the seventh grade, he mixed with students who were significantly older and more mature. If you were a boy, it meant trying to make as few waves as possible. I did just that.

For me the work at the junior/senior high school level was twice as challenging as elementary school, and I had no resources, no magic to help me with my reading, writing, and math. I had almost no accomplishments of any kind in school those years with one inexplicable exception. In grade school I could not answer a question as simple as "If you have a quarter and an apple is a nickel. How many can you buy?" Yet when I took algebra, geometry, and trigonometry. I had success. In fact, my teachers thought I was cheating. Short of this success though, all I had to look forward to was failure each and every day. My only other attainments lay in my hobby of working with wood. I liked making things and creating objects from unusual materials. Most of this work found its way into my room at home. I also discovered I had the ability to use certain tools and materials other than what was typically required. For example, drawing and painting were difficult for me, so I would paste colored paper on my drawing of a building to get the desired effect. This kind of work was my first experience with alternate thinking and going outside the box.

SCHOOL DAYS

Although handicapped, I was not a slacker. *I did not want to be a failure.* I wanted to become something in life, and I always tried to master the subjects I was taking. I would go home and study and try to learn the material I was responsible for. I developed my own pattern of study. Since I did not actually have a desk yet at this time, I would use the dining room table and convert it into my personal space. I squirreled away all the accessories that I thought should be on a desk and each night of school, I would take out my pens, pencils, erasers, and assorted paraphernalia and sit down for work. That was my routine, but the results were almost always the same. In junior and senior high school there were not any Mr. Kleins. There were more formidable teachers whose tolerance for a handicapped student was nil. On top of that, I also had the experience of sharing teachers my brothers had. This did not always work out for me, as I discovered on more than one occasion. In particular one teacher went as far as to say in so many words I was going to pay for the sins of my brothers. I did not take this lightly and had the temerity to see the principal and explain the circumstances. He changed my class.

Like elementary school, I made many friends in high school. Friends for life. Despite the fact there were many cliques, it was easy for someone to move from one to another. I did just that and I simply bounced from group to group. However, the people on my street were my first friends: Johnny Stiles, Herb Kaufman, Richie Marks, and Jerry Dalven. After them, it was Bob Governale, Marty Starr, or Meyer Modlin. Each one of these friends circulated in different groups yet they were still friendly with me. In addition, there were also my summer friends, those who came out for the summer and returned to the city in the fall.

I had friends among this group also. It was simple: if you lived in Long Beach, it meant you had many friends and each one was unique in his own way. Take Meyer Modlin, for example. He marched to his own drumbeat. Independent and loyal, a rebel in many ways. No man or boy could want a more committed and supportive friend. I have been lucky. He has been my friend for life. In high school, I discovered girls, and I dated many of them. I was not shy about girls. Some I went out with for longer times than others. I only had what could be called one serious relationship. Socially, I had found a comfort zone. For me, my friends, whether male or female, were neither any better nor any worse than I was. I accepted them as they were. This egalitarian mind-set became a strength of mine; although I certainly was not aware of it at the time. It has served me well through life.

During these years, one of my favorite pastimes in the summer was to take my father's powerboat out onto Reynold's Channel and race other boats. Our course was generally a series of buoys we raced around. There were always kids there looking for a challenge. Perhaps our racing fever was brought on by the yearly formal races on the bay. These races were held in various categories. The most spectacular category was the unlimited hydroplanes. These boats brought in huge throngs of people to watch them perform. They also brought celebrities like Guy Lombardo who drove his own hydroplane. Surplus World War II Allison aircraft engines of

---

15. *"I wish I was to the sphere, as I am to the circle."*

more than 1,000 horsepower powered the hydroplanes. As they soared down Reynold's Channel, I would watch as huge rooster tails of water were thrown up into the air and the roar of their exhausts reverberated from one end of town to the other. I eventually borrowed a smaller version of one of these boats that I raced in the lesser events. There was a joy and a freedom to those days on the water, and it was everything that school was not for me.

While going through high school, I worked every summer in Long Beach. If I could find a way, I always worked for myself. I preferred that because I feared my disability would get in the way of any other job I might work at. One of my business enterprises was to buy soda in the supermarket for five cents and then go out onto Reynold's Channel in my rowboat and sell that same soda for fifteen cents. When I wasn't doing something like that, I was a beachcomber or a slinger of hamburgers or a manager of a children's park. When I was seventeen, I bought a custard stand. It was my first deal. It happened when the owner died and his wife accepted my offer to be paid for the business on a weekly basis out of the proceeds. What I confirmed from this experience is that I enjoyed making money and that I knew how to save it as well as spend it.

I had to leave Long Beach High School in my senior year because I was in danger of not graduating. My family expected me to go to college and obviously graduation from high school was a prerequisite. Thus, I was sent to Cheshire Academy in Connecticut for my final year.

Cheshire felt like a prison to me. It was the same experience as Long Beach only in a private setting and without girls. It was not surprising that I did not have as many friends there as in Long Beach. It was a different kind of school. Many of the boys who attended classes there were troubled, but nonetheless, I did make one good friend. Tom Dodd. He and I were outsiders by virtue of the fact that we were not like the majority of students. I was not uncomfortable being on the outside, and I learned to cope in this new and unfamiliar situation. While I was at Cheshire, I had one great success. Fencing. Saber. It was my only sport. I was one of the best at the sport, and I defeated everyone I faced. My success at fencing was a wonderful experience for me. It made me aware of the things I could do, not only the things I could not do. When I won my most important match of the year for the school championship, my self-esteem surfaced with a jolt that I had not had in many, many years.

I was only at Cheshire for that one year. Aside from all the fights and male aggression that were integral to the school, the teachers were largely misfits. Generally, they were castoffs from public educational programs or untrained hires filling a teaching void. Once one of my teachers at Cheshire sent home a test paper to my mother. My grade was a thirty. His letter accused me of not studying. I took exception to his criticism and made an appointment to see the principal. When I met with him, I explained I was doing my best. The principal called in my teacher and asked him about my work. The teacher's reply was, "Of course, you are right. The note never should have been sent. In order for him to receive a thirty, he had to study. Otherwise, he would have received a zero."

In spite of my difficulties, I graduated Cheshire, but I did not receive a diploma for my academic work. Graduation from Chesire was more about a contractual obligation to its students than earning a degree.

During my final years in high school, one of my closest friends was Jerry Dalven. I first met him when his house was being built at the end of our street. Jerry was older than I was, and he was very bright. The difference in our intellects was never an issue between us. We just liked one another. When it was time to apply for college, something seemingly impossible to me, Jerry stepped in to help. My thinking was that a career as a carpenter seemed like a good life given my talents. I told my mother of this one day, and she was outraged that I would make such a choice. At that precise moment, Jerry walked into my house. He shared my mother's viewpoint. The next day he sat down with me and went through a list of professions from A to Z. We never got past A. When Jerry explained to me what an architect did for a living, I decided that would be just the thing for me. I ignored the fact that my grades were horrid, my reading, writing, and math skills were poor, and the daunting demands of an architecture program. I just knew it was right for me and from that day on I determined that no matter what obstacles I had to overcome, I would be an architect. Jerry was an integral part of that decision.

Soon, I was applying to colleges. Jerry helped me with the applications. I never took the SAT. I figured I'd do poorly and that on top of my lousy academic record would spell an end to my college hopes. It was not long before I realized that SAT or no SAT, I was going to have a tough time getting into any college. I sent many applications. All but one was rejected. For some unknown reason, Tulane University in New Orleans, Louisiana, accepted me. Sometimes, I believe

I was accepted to their School of Architecture because Tulane wanted students from the East coast and a Jewish presence. However, when I reflect on my acceptance now, I think someone simply made a mistake.

I liked Tulane and I loved New Orleans, but I disliked the South. There was segregation then: full blown and mean. Trolley cars were a blatant example of this discrimination. Whites were given the first choice to the seats in the front of the cars. As the seats were filled by whites, blacks had to move to the rear of the cars. In some cases, all the seats would be occupied by whites regardless of who was on the trolley first. It was ugly business and none of us from the north liked it very much. I recall one incident in particular. Two soldiers entered the trolley, one black and the other white. They probably were on leave from Fort Polk, Louisiana. Both were bedecked with medals and campaign ribbons from the Korean War. They sat side by side, taking the first two seats they saw. The conductor turned to them and said in a less than friendly voice "Blacks to the rear." As the black soldier rose to comply, the white soldier pulled him back down into his seat. The trolley car driver turned again and this time he snarled, "Niggers to the rear." Once again, the black soldier tried to go to the rear and was restrained by his friend. Then, the conductor rose from his seat and walked toward the two soldiers. He stopped before the black soldier and said, "Nigger, I told you to get in the back! If there are no seats, get off my trolley." In an instant, almost too fast to see, the white soldier leaped from his seat and began to pummel the conductor. Who fell back toward the front of the trolley. Finally, the conductor, badly beaten, fell out of the trolley

SCHOOL DAYS

door to the street where the beating continued before a large crowd, which had gathered to witness the mayhem. When the police finally arrived, they broke the light up and called the military police. As fate would have it, the two military policemen were both black. Another night I was working at night in the architecture building on Tulane's campus. A fellow student from Shreveport, Louisiana, came into the room where I was drawing. He said, "Hi, Al, how are you?"

"Fine."

"Here you are working on a Saturday night."

"Yup, I have work to do."

"Hey, why don't you come with me? A truckload of us are going out to kick some nigger's ass."

"Not for me. That's not my sport." He left without a word.

While at Tulane, I worked very hard but to no avail. I couldn't even maintain a C average. In my third year, I was called in by the dean of the School of Architecture. He advised me that I had two choices: to resign or be flunked out. It seemed my college career was all over for me. I felt enormous disappointment. It didn't make a difference which choice I made, I was finished and so was my dream. The dean convinced me to resign, suggesting that if I ever wanted to go to a school again, at least I would have a chance. It was a fortuitous suggestion although I did not know it then. So I left Tulane. Humbled by my failure, I remained in the South for a while and eventually returned home for the summer. I went to work then for the architect Donald Bailey. I enjoyed working for him and did well at my job. One day in August, he asked me when I was returning to school. I explained to him that I wasn't. Then, I told him what had happened. He listened sympathetically and asked me what I wanted. I told him I wanted my degree. Then, he suggested that I sign up for night courses at Columbia University as a non-matriculated student. He was familiar with Columbia because he was on their admissions board. I followed his advice and took the courses while working for him during the day. I succeeded in my two courses and received Bs. Then, in a moment of good luck, I was contacted by a high school friend, Jim McMullen. He was attending the University of Kansas as an architecture student and suggested I apply there. I took his advice and to my complete surprise. I was accepted. The stipulation was that I had three years of work to do at Kansas to satisfy the school's requirements. I felt that was more than fair given that architecture was a five-year program. I joined Kansas at an important time for the institution. Wilt Chamberlin had also arrived and would put Kansas on the collegiate map.

Once there, I worked as hard as I could. I knew this was my last chance. I availed myself of all sources of help available. Friends were a big part of it, and more than one of them assisted me over the difficult spots.

Roger Kaster was probably one of the most influential people among this group. He was a farm boy from Kansas who never met a New Yorker or a Jew before me, and I was a Jewish New Yorker who had never met a farm boy from Kansas. I grew to love Roger. He was a genuine and moral human being.

After Kansas, I lost track of Roger Kaster. Years went by, and I was deep into my career and working with various banks and insurance companies on some very large projects. One of the insurance companies was MONY. As I was closing a deal with them in their New York City offices for a forty-million-dollar loan, I noticed two architectural renderings on the wall of the office complex. I liked their look and asked where they were being built. The MONY official replied "Kansas City." I asked who the architect was and he answered, "Roger Caster." I gasped. After further inquiries by me, it turned out that Roger was MONY's man in the Midwest and that his talents were widely employed by them.

I asked for Roger's phone number and called him. It was a wonderful chat, and we resumed our friendship then and have kept it ever since. I did well in my classes at Kansas. My grades were all C or better. At the end of my third year, however, I was told by the registrar that certain courses from Tulane would not be approved and graduation would not occur. That meant I had to return for another year. This made me quite angry. I felt Kansas had breached our agreement. I went home that Christmas and pondered how I could solve this problem. Finally, I realized that because I was from New York and my father was in the millinery business, everyone at Kansas thought I was a millionaire. I had tried to explain otherwise in the past, but no one paid much attention to what I said. Now, I decided I could use that perception to my advantage. When I returned to school after vacation, I made an appointment to see the dean of the School of Architecture. I entered his office and took a chair opposite him.

"Good morning."

"Good morning, Allen."

"You know, I talked to my parents about Kansas when I was home. I told them how much I have loved my time here and that no other college I have attended has been as good to me. My parents were impressed, and they told me they would like to make a sizable donation to the school to thank you for all your help. They asked me to find out how they could make such a donation, and they would like to make it in your name." I could see he felt immensely flattered by what I was saying.

"Of course we'll help. I'll get you all the necessary forms and contact your mother also."

"Well, that might be a bit premature, sir. You see, they want to make the donation after I graduate. They wouldn't want to exert any undue influence on my work while I am still a student at Kansas."

"Well, Allen, when do you graduate?"

"My transcript has to be evaluated. I have to make sure all my grades are accepted from my other schools."

"We can do that right now, Allen." His secretary pulled my records, and as I sat there, he went over my transcripts. In a short while he looked up at me and smiled. "Everything is in order, Allen. You'll be graduating this year. No problem."

"Great, my folks will be here for graduation, and they'll have a check for you." With that, I rose, shook his hand, and left the room.

Of course, my parents didn't know a thing, nor did they have the requisite money. As it turned out, my father could not attend graduation, only my mother. I had no plans to tell her anything. On the fateful day, my mother was sitting there bursting with pride. I sat with my heart beating wildly until my name was called. Then, I walked up and received my diploma from the dean. He winked at me as he placed the treasured document in my hand, and I winked back. Immediately, I went to where my mother was sitting. I had made arrangements to hustle her out of there without delay. Since I was one of the last to receive his diploma, I knew the dean would be hunting us down. I grabbed my mother by the hand and took her to a secluded spot. I could see the dean searching for us, and I was desperate to leave. It seemed like hours before my friend Roger, who was in on my scam, pulled up in his car. I told my mom I had to rush into Kansas City for a huge party and could not remain. She accepted my explanation, and we fled the campus.

I felt as if I had just completed the longest journey of my life. A twenty-year academic odyssey, where my chances of survival, were about on par with those of Odysseus. But I made it. Now, life awaited me.

Making It

After I returned home from Kansas, I went back to work for the local architect, Donald Bailey, the one that got me into Columbia. Donald was a good man who had helped me many times in the past and would help me many times in the future. When I went to work for him, I started at $35 a week. It was not quite what I had in mind for my life's work, but I had no better option at the time and so I worked hard at my craft and tried to learn as much as I could. Learning as much as I could meant dealing with local builders and drawing plans for them. On one occasion a builder, someone I did not know, came into the office. He was wearing dirty overalls, had a toothpick in his mouth, and carried a greasy lunch bag. He slapped a drawing of a house on my desk and asked me to draw plans from the sketch. It was a house he wanted to build. I told him his plans would be ready by the weekend. After he left, I looked more closely at his rendering of the house. His concept was ludicrous. The man hadn't a clue about design. Therefore, I decided to make a few changes to improve on his elemental plan. A few days later when I proudly presented his revised plan, he reacted with anger. He said what I did was not what he wanted and was unacceptable. His design was exactly what he wanted. So I redrew the plan according to his concept. He returned for his version of the home, and when I gave him his drawings, he was visibly pleased. After he left, I shook my head in wonder at both his ignorance and his success. Three months later he returned. This time he wanted five more sets of the same plan. He explained he had five more plots, and he wanted the exact design duplicated. I stayed up all night preparing the home and site plans. I called him when I finished and told him his plans were ready. He came in the next day, accepted the plans, and gave me a check for them. Then, he left. When I saw my employer, Don Bailey, I handed him the builder's check. Then, I told him, "I quit."

As I packed my architectural equipment and prepared to leave, my boss said, "See you on Monday."

I replied, "No, I am really quitting. For good." He looked at me with astonishment and amazement as I left the building.

When I drew the builder's plans the previous night, I had an epiphany. Here, I was working for $35 a week while the builder sold six homes, made $30,000 with lousy house plans, and would be spending the winter in Florida vacationing. Although I did not have a dime in my pocket, I decided I could do better as a builder. I had a strong work ethic, and I threw myself into my career and worked as hard as I ever had in my life.

I knew I needed land to build a house. I wanted to build in Long Beach because this was the area I knew best. As it turned out, Donald Bailey owned two plots of land,

16. *"Unbridled passion can make us vulnerable to rejection."*

and they were available. One was in Long Beach and the other was in Island Park, just over the bridge connecting Long Beach to Long Island. The only way I could view the Island Park property was by boat. At the time there was no road access to it. So, I took my old boat and went with Don Bailey to view the land. It was a fine piece of property right on Reynold's Channel. Instinctively, I knew waterfront property would always have great value and even though it was inaccessible, I knew I was going to buy it. The other property was located on Boyd Street at the east end of Long Beach in an area known as "The Canals." "The Canals" were so named because canals had been dredged to give homeowner's access to Reynold's Channel. The property instantly became valuable for anyone who wanted the water and a boat at his front door. Homes sprung up along these canals like mushrooms. The plot on Boyd Street was not very large. It was fifty feet wide and eighty feet deep. Nonetheless, I decided this piece of land would be the location of my first home. It was a gutsy decision since I knew almost nothing about the intricacies of financing and constructing a home nor did I have $5,000 for the land. All I had was my ability to design a home and my faith in myself. Donald Bailey knew about my financial situation, and he was kind enough to wait on me and not sell the land to someone else while I raised the money. Before I tackled the money issue, however, I thought it best to design the house. Once I finished the design, I decided to look for investors. I went to friends and family members and just about anyone else I thought might be interested in investing. My promise to them was their original investment back plus a piece of the profits for them.

My powers of persuasion were good enough for me to raise the $5,000 Donald Bailey wanted for the land.

Armed with the property as my principal asset, I now needed a building loan to begin work on the house. For this, I chose to go to a local bank. Central Federal Savings. Central Federal was run and owned by a native of Long Beach, Teddy Ornstein. At one time, Teddy had been the mayor of Long Beach and he knew just about everyone in town, and everyone in town knew him. This included my family. Based on that familiarity, it seemed perfectly logical that it was him I should see. Therefore, I met with him and the result of that meeting was a building loan. Armed with new money, I went out with the intention of hiring someone to build my house. What I didn't realize is that many, many trades were involved in the building of a home, from concrete men to roofers and everything in between. It was an awakening of sorts, and it was a costly lesson for me. I learned about who and what was needed to build a house and the importance of getting the people in the proper sequence and on schedule so the next tradesman could follow. Because I did not know these things before my venture into the building world, interest rates piled up as construction slowed down due to poor scheduling on my part. It was a mistake I never made again. The house I constructed was a "modern" design. It was built from Texture III, a kind of exterior grooved plywood that gave a rustic, rugged look. Texture III also had a good reputation for durability and strength. The house was a ranch with a side entrance due to the size of the plot. There were three bedrooms, two bathrooms, a living room, dining room, and kitchen. The home's one special feature was an entrance courtyard, which allowed open access to all the living areas in the house. I finally finished the house and put it up for sale. My price was $13,000. It was 1961. Finally, after what seemed forever, a broker walked into my house and told me he had a buyer. I sold the house on Boyd Street for a slight loss, but I sold it and that was the most important thing. Before I sold the home, I used one of the bedrooms as a workspace. There was an empty lot behind the house, and since I had no pressing business on hand, I decided to design a home for that property. I ignored the fact that I did not own the land. I was still working in the room on my new design a few weeks before occupancy when a couple walked in looking for me. They were a husband and a wife. The husband spoke.

"Is Mr. Weinstein here?"

"Yes, he is," I replied.

"Oh, no, is Mr. Weinstein here?"

"Yes. I am he."

"Oh, well is your father here?"

"If you want hats, you can call my father. If you want a house, you speak to me."

"I hope you aren't insulted. You seem quite young to be a builder. We saw this house from the street and are interested in it. Is it for sale?"

"No, I am sorry, but it has been sold."

"Oh, what is that?" He pointed to my drawing board and the house plan I was designing.

17. *"In life we shed our past and undergo rebirth. The only constant is our soul."*

Without missing a beat, I said, "The house I am building on that lot." I nodded my head toward the property behind my house.

"You are going to build it?"

"Yup."

"Can we look at the plan more closely?"

"Sure."

"It's a very interesting home. Do you think we might take the plans home to study a bit further?

"Sure. No problem. Call me if you have any questions.

The house the couple was looking at was what I called an "H" house. The entrance was separated from the living room by a fireplace. To the left were the bedrooms and to the right was the dining room and kitchen. Apparently, the husband and wife liked it because they called me in a few days later and asked me to build the house for them. I agreed. My only problem now was that I did not own the lot. They asked me when we could go to contract, and I stalled them as best I could by saying I wouldn't be free until I cleaned up my current business. This bought me some time. The task for me now was to find the landowner and find some financing. I immediately found the owner and asked him his price. He said, "$6,000," and it was mine. I only had $4,500 remaining from my first deal, and I went to the same people again for financing and despite the poor return on their investment for the first home, they supported me. Now, I had my land, and I had some experience and I was ready to build house #2. While I was building #2, a road was built to the land Donald Bailey was holding for me in Island Park. Now, this water locked property suddenly had considerable value. I designed a house for the property and placed it on the market. Given its location, I knew the house would sell as soon as it was on the market. I was feeling good about my building projects and about my future prospects when an old high school friend approached me. He had learned I was building homes and was interested in a home for himself. He asked me to draw plans for him because he had seen the homes I was building, and he liked my designs. As a favor to him, I drew the plans. He loved the house and told me how he was going to build it on land his father gave him. After he put the house out for bid, he came to me again.

"Al, do you think a price of $21,000 is fair for building your design."

"Well, the house costs the builder $15,000 to $16,000. He's making about $5,000 profit. That is fair in today's market."

"It seems like a lot to me. I'm kind of cash strapped." He studied me for a moment and then asked, "Why can't we build it instead? As friends."

"What do you mean by that?" I asked.

"Well, look, you sign a contract with me. I'll go to the bank and get a building loan. I'll do everything. I get the contractors and supervise the job. You won't have to do a thing. I'll be on it every day, but I need your name on the contract to get the loan."

Out of friendship and his apparent sincerity, I accepted his offer. I was not going to get a thing from working with him other than the $75 I charged him for my plans. After the building loan was obtained with my help and signed by me personally, I found he had disappeared, and I was solely in charge of the construction site and the building of the house.

The only time I saw him during the construction phase was when he came to me to complain about one thing or another. Since I now had a loan to pay, I pushed the project forward as rapidly as possible to lower interest debt.

I finally finished the home and the total cost was $16,500, $500 over the contract. I told him I needed the $500 to square our accounts. He said, "No. The contract was for $16,000 and that is the deal." I looked at him with incredulity. I did not know whether to throw him out the nearest window or tell him exactly what I felt. I did neither. What I did do is never speak to him again although he has wanted to see me over the years. I have never taken the time to contact him. Nor have I ever used this incident as a warning sign in my dealings with other people. Over the decades I have been burnt many times, but the good people outweigh those who would take advantage.

After his house was completed, I had four homes under my belt and some money in the bank. I was a young unmarried guy with $10,000 in his bank account. Not too shabby for those days. In addition, I had learned much about the business of being a builder. I still did not have my own workplace. Instead, I was using Donald Bailey's architectural office as my base, and in return, I did bits and pieces of work for him in payment for the space I used. One day as I was finishing some plans up for Donald, a man walked into the

18. *"Listen to a man's words, but give his actions more value before you give him respect."*

office. He was wearing a black jacket, a black turtleneck sweater, and black pants. He was a medium-sized man, slim, and good-looking. He introduced himself as Walter Penn and shook my hand and Donald Bailey's.

"I have a plot of land in Atlantic Beach, and I'm in the market for a house. I want a house designed and built for me, Mr. Bailey.

"I'm not a residential builder, Mr. Penn. I do commercial projects."

"Oh, then I guess I have come to the wrong place."

"No. There's your man right there." Donald pointed at me.

"Do you build houses? You seem pretty young."

"I am a builder and an architect."

"OK. That's good. Can you show me some of your work?"

I took out the plans for the houses I had built and showed them to him before I asked him to view the property. His response was favorable, and I drove to the lot with Mr. Penn in tow. The property was a beautiful piece close to where the bay emptied into the ocean, but it was located in an area favored by some alleged New York City mobsters. I felt compelled to ask him if he was aware of the reputation of his neighbors. He said he didn't care about things like that. I went ahead and designed a very modern home with large open spaces and high ceilings. Mr. Penn, as I called him, would be out at the job site almost every day in a chauffeured black limo. He invariably would get out come up to me, put his arm around

19. *"Dreams are as real as we make them, and the more we believe in them, the more attainable they become."*

my shoulder, and asked, "OK, how much of the contract do you think you did today? $300?"

"Probably," I'd reply.

He'd peel the money off a roll and hand it to me and say, "Take it off the contract." It was that way with almost everything. Once, I recall taking him to Center Millwork to have his custom kitchen cabinets made. The price for the work was $2,000. After Mr. Penn paid the Millwork for the cabinets, he pulled me aside as we were leaving and stuffed $185 in my hand.

"That's for your help." I was stunned. All I had done was drive him to the mill and here I was being given a week's wages, if not more.

A few more months went by, and Mr. Penn's house was all but ready for occupancy. Only the shrubs remained to be done. On the day the landscaper arrived, I was there. I watched as he unloaded his truck and prepared the holes for the various trees and plantings. About this time, Mr. Penn drove up in his limo. When he stepped from the vehicle, I could see he was agitated.

"What are you doing?"

"I'm giving you your landscaping."

"No. No. No. You can't do the landscaping. My brother-in-law is a landscaper, and if I don't give him the business, my wife will have my head."

"But you already paid for it. It's in the contract."

"That's OK. No problem."

"OK."

I went over to the landscaper and explained what had happened. He took it very well, telling me he could use the trees and shrubs on another job. He then returned the money I had given him for the job. I gave the money to Mr. Penn, and once again he gave me 20% of the money for my work.

For all intents and purposes the house was done, and I delivered it to Mr. Penn. I asked him to call me when the house was landscaped because I wanted to take photos. He assured me he would call. The days, weeks, and months went by; and he never called. I felt badly about it because I had a genuine affection for Mr. Penn and always felt in his debt for the way he treated me. Time passed and Mr. Penn was far from my thoughts as I read *Newsday*, Long Island's paper, one fine spring morning. An article's title caught my eye, "Mobster Killed."

The story went on to relate how Walter Penn, a mob hit man, had been gunned down. I suddenly understood his aversion to shrubs.

My name and work had become familiar to brokers by now, and I was having people referred to me. As I met with these potential customers, I began a large new home on Bay Boulevard adjacent to Reynold's Channel. This home featured an interior courtyard as its central feature. It also had many large windows and sliding door units facing the bay. I quickly found buyers who were thrilled with the design. While I was working on this home, another couple came in to see me. They wanted a home built in the sand dune area of Lido Beach at the east end of Long Beach on a very narrow plot of land. They wanted the house high enough so that the ocean could be viewed. Such a structure would be unique in Lido Beach or anywhere. I began work on the structure almost immediately. I was rising 6:30 in the morning and working to 8:30 at night building these two homes.

Being a builder was time and energy consuming. How much more I could do, I asked myself, than this? And what does someone do who builds fifty houses? Suddenly, it dawned on me that the effort to build two homes could be applied to building 50. I decided in that instant that I would never build single homes again, and from that day on, I started to look for larger pieces of property. Following that decision, I got in my car, a Volkswagen, and I drove out to eastern Long Island. I started to see brokers and inquire about enough land to build fifty homes. The brokers thought I was an eccentric millionaire since I drove a Volkswagen while trying to buy fifty acres of land. I followed this routine for several months. Most of the property was too expensive for me. Then, opportunity presented itself to me. I was taken by a broker, Leo Lang, to see 207 acres of land for sale in Ridge, New York. The price was a thousand dollars an acre. Lange said I could get terms, "builder's terms." I didn't let on that I hadn't a clue about what he was talking about, and I left him with the idea that I was interested in the property. With that I rushed off to find out about the mysterious "builder's terms." I knew Harold Bailey, Donald's uncle, a lawyer and real estate dealer would have the answers I needed. He did. "Builder's terms" meant that a builder paid 29% of the price. The remainder was in a mortgage. The reason the amount was 29% and not 30% was that taxes did not have to be paid on the land until all the money for the work had been collected. The 29% was considered an installment. So now I had to raise almost $60,000 for the land. I started a campaign to raise investors. I printed a prospectus for distribution, I buttonholed people, I talked, cajoled, and charmed anyone and everyone who could be a potential investor in my dream. While I was doing all of this, I lost contact with Leo Lange. Leo Lange had not forgotten me though, and after he had not heard from me for some time, he called.

"Hi, Alan. How are you?"

"Fine."

"I haven't heard from you in some time."

"I've been pretty busy."

"I was wondering if you are still interested in the Ridge property?"

"Yeah. Sure."

"Well, I was thinking the price was a bit steep when I didn't hear from you. So, I spoke to the owner, and you can have the land for $750 an acre."

"That's great. Thanks. I'll get back to you within a few days,"

I was elated. Now, all I needed was $45,000 instead of $60,000. I raised the money in short order from twelve investors and the 207 acres were mine. The deal I made with my investors was that they divided 70% of the profit after their investment was paid back. I received the other 30% of the profits.

I sat with the land for one year. I could not raise any more money until I proved myself with my first investment, and I was uncertain how to proceed. So I diddled about doing odd jobs for Harold Bailey and running a small boardwalk business I had acquired. I also kept looking for land opportunities and waiting for something to break. I was still in this mode when

I received a call from Joe Oppenheimer, one of the largest real estate brokers on Long Island.

"Hello, Allen. This is Joe Oppenheimer."

"Yes?"

"Do you want to sell your land out on the island?"

"Sure. Which piece?" Of course I only had one piece of property, but I didn't want Joe Oppenheimer to know that.

"The one you have in Ridge."

"Well, we weren't thinking of selling it, but for the right price, sure."

"House Beautiful is interested in it and will buy it from you." I knew House Beautiful was one of the largest builders on Long Island at the time, and I tried to keep a clear head and not give in to excitement as we talked.

"Have they made an offer?"

"They'll pay you $1,500 an acre." My mind played with the numbers for a moment. A $750 profit per acre for over two hundred acres and all the money I had invested to that date was $45,000, a small percentage of the overall worth of the property.

"I can do that deal."

"OK, Allen. I'll get back to you with details."

I sold the piece within weeks. My investors had put in $5,000 each. They received $12,000 as a return on their investment, and they were ecstatic. Within weeks following the sale, I literally needed two people to answer my phone. Calls from them and from their friends clamoring for new deals in which they could become involved were seemingly endless. I had become an overnight sensation and people wanted in. I was now a land syndicator and would become one of the biggest on Long Island. Opportunity, luck, determination, salesmanship, talent, and courage had brought me to a place I had only dreamed about as a child. I was a long way from the kid who was last in his class.

20. *"Gather all the wisdom of the universe as we travel through space and time, and make it a part of our journey here on this small planet."*

Notes

Sweet Smell of Success

I was in need of a partner. As it turned out, my lawyer Harold Bailey had reached a stage in his life where he decided to step back somewhat from the tumult of the business world. This would leave his son Dick with the bulk of their work. When I heard about Harold's decision, I was pleased to think I would now be working with Dick on a more exclusive basis. Dick had always been a hero of mine and someone I greatly admired. The timing was perfect for each of us. Consequently, we formed a partnership that lasted for almost twenty years. We built homes in Oceanside, Plainview, and a host of other locations on Long Island. My role in our partnership was to find suitable land for construction projects. Dick handled the construction. As time passed, we became partners with Island Park Plumbing and Heating, a local firm that we dealt with in the construction of homes. Our new alliance extended the range of our involvement with construction. With this new capability in mind, PSI Inc. was formed to build sewage treatment plants. The company eventually went public. Our new corporation soon became a major player in the construction of several treatment plants on Long Island.

Subsequently, we became involved with the design and the development of the Henry Ford Plantation, Artist Lake, and the Villas in Plainview. One other partner was involved in all of this work, my brother Joe. Although Joe is nine years older than I, it has never affected a partnership that has existed for more than four decades. Through all the years, we have experienced the roller coaster ride of the business world together, enjoying the ups and suffering through the downs. Our roles in our business ventures have been different, but we have complemented one another's strengths.

Having Joe as a partner, a friend, and a brother through all these years has been a gift I shall always treasure. There has never been a business deal that I was involved with which did not involve Joe. With Joe, I always felt from day one that my back was covered. It has never been otherwise. Suffice to say in all our time together, we have never experienced a major disagreement or returned home at night angry over a business dispute. As we built our businesses, most of the major impediments we faced were with building inspectors. However, acquiring building permits took very little time since environmental issues were almost nonexistent. Another saving grace was that the banks were easy to deal with during these years. (Too easy, as I was to learn). It became axiomatic that as long as we handled our building loans properly, we had few difficulties.

In my career, my philosophy was always to keep many irons in the fire at the same time. I knew I couldn't rely on any one project. I never locked myself into a singularity. Moreover, once I wanted a deal, I made it happen. I was relentless. I knew every detail of a potential deal, as well as all the pitfalls and advantages. Before I went to any meeting, I made certain I understood how far I could go, and when

I had to walk, I took the time to find out what the road situation was and if water and other utilities were available. I never was caught unprepared in this way; although there were always surprises of one kind or another. Because I have a way of understanding both sides of a deal, I knew what I needed, and I knew what the other person needed. I priced my offer for land by learning what I could build on the property. Next, I calculated how much it would cost to improve the land. Following that I determined what it cost me to build, what houses sold for in the area, and if the profit margin was large enough. I never tried to fool or trick anyone.

When I was buying a building, my policy was to look at all the income. I checked leases and rentals and whether rent was increasing or decreasing. I projected the future to determine the percentage of vacancy and all my maintenance expenses.

Expenses such as improvements were always factored in. I never bought a building that I did not improve. In one development I owned, every apartment needed improvement. There were 1,300 apartments, but I always believed renovations meant making money, not losing money. Therefore, whether it was twenty apartments or 1,300, I applied my philosophy of the worth of renovations.

As my business grew, I learned it's difficult to be loyal when making a deal. It was much easier not to be. There were many temptations to lead one astray. I tried to avoid those temptations. I understood I was dealing with the money of others and in a fiduciary position. In the all the years of my business life, I never had a nasty letter from an investor or bank. My mantra was to never misappropriate money entrusted to me. Much in the same way, I have always been loyal to those who have been good to me. During the bad times, many people stood up for me. I have never forgotten who they were and I remain true to them to this very day. Loyalty to me also meant paying one hundred cents on a dollar to my subcontractors. Many builders would have a bill and pay only a part of it. If a job was billed at $50,000, when the contractor came in for payment, a builder might only offer $45,000. Generally, the contractor would take the money because to sue meant paying a lawyer and a concomitant loss of time and work. Although contractors often went to work again for the very same builders who shorted them, I never conducted my business that way. I had many bad times, but I never tried to settle my responsibilities by hurting those whom I owed money.

During the Franklin disaster, I had just finished a job in Oceanside. I was also doing a turnkey job in Long Beach, the first in New York State for low-cost housing, and had completed a shopping center and was receiving good income from it. I had cash in the bank, but I was always working, and running with never a moment's rest. Moreover, I always was digging out of trouble. Everything came back into my lap. As I said earlier, it was at this time I considered an alternate career. I was burned out or close to it. Teaching seemed like a very good idea to me then. All of that changed when I returned from vacation, and my hard won fortune was lost in Franklin's crash.

21. *"Hurt can only occur if there is intent, otherwise it is a misperception."*

SWEET SMELL OF SUCCESS

After Franklin failed, it was more than five years of hand-to-mouth survival. To say my partners and I were in bad shape would be an understatement, but what I always preserved were my name and reputation. Nonetheless, now my office was in the basement of my brother's home and prospects did not look good for us. When a builder named Abe Shames contacted me, Abe called himself "Uncle Abe." As it turned out, he was not very avuncular. Abe invited me and my partners to move into his office in Bethpage. He said he would obtain all the money to complete Artist Lake and the Villas of Plainview. He explained that he would go to the bank, raise the money, and become a business partner. His ostensible reason for wanting to join with me was that he had sons, I had a good reputation, and he wanted his sons working with me. At the time I still owned several hundred acres of land in Yaphank, Long Island, and banks were interested in my expertise in doing deals and they were interested in the potential of my land. So I was valuable to them and to others. Abe knew about my property, its inherent value, and he wanted it for himself. Clearly, his interest had nothing to do with his sons. His thinking was that I would lose the property because of my financial problems, but he was wrong. I was fighting tooth and nail against that ever happening, and no one fights harder than I do. One day Abe said to me, "Why don't you give your land to Uncle Abe, and I will protect it for you, and then when you are out of trouble, I'll sign it back to you." Of course there was no way I was signing my land over to him. I found his offer rude and insulting, but I never let him know. That would not have been good business. Nonetheless, we did have offices in his building, and he did obtain some money as a loan for our projects from Meadowbrook Bank, and he said he was going to get more. Thus, as an incentive for him to help us, he kept pushing for me to sign my land over to him. When I would demur, he would say, "Don't you trust me? Maybe we shouldn't do this job? Maybe you shouldn't be in the office. I am trying to protect you from the creditors. I'll hold the land for you. Not to worry."

I listened but did not respond. I had a big problem. I needed Abe's office space to conduct business. I had no other place to go. I also needed the little money Abe obtained for us to help with the Villas and Artist Lake while I was fighting the Franklin case. I was in a quandary about what to do. Then, one night, an idea presented itself to me. The next day, I went to Abe's office, and I signed over the deeds. There was a great deal of paperwork associated with the deeds and the papers were spread out all over his desk. It was quite confusing and that was the way I wanted it. When Abe finally signed the deed, a smile of satisfaction crossed his face. He was positively ebullient to finally have his hands on my treasure. What Abe did not realize when he signed the deed was that he signed two sets.

While I did give him the deeds, unknowingly, he had deeded the same land back to me by signing the second set. He had no idea that he had been snookered. Our deal was for Abe to just hold the property aside until I was ready to reclaim it. Instead of honoring that agreement, Abe filed the deeds and offered my property as collateral for bank loans. I was angry at his perfidy, but I knew I did not need Abe in the least. I could have gone to the bank on my own without him. I just never wanted to do that. My response to Abe's betrayal was swift. I filed my deeds. Before the bank gave him any money, they did a search and discovered the land was mine. To put it mildly, Abe was stunned. He knew he had been outsmarted by me, and needless to say, this created a rift between us and we split.

When I last saw him, he vented his anger at me. I replied, "Don't yell at me. You are the crook. You put up the land for collateral and you were not supposed to."

He replied, "Well, what did you think I was going to do?"

"You're a liar," I said. "I thought you were going to hold the land for me as you said. Why do I need you as my partner if my land is being used for collateral?" Uncle Abe's florid face flushed with anger. He had been outfoxed. Beaten at his own game and he did not like it very much, he struck back in the only way he knew how. He threw me out of his building. Now. I had my land back, but I had no office. Without a place to work, my brother Joe and I once again appropriated his basement for our new office. It was not exactly Kensington Palace. No heat. No air. Two desks. Two chairs. Lamps.

We started to think about an offer that would have us going into the insulation business, but the deal didn't work out. We concluded if nothing further presented itself, we were going to sell our homes and relocate. Quite simply put, we were broke, and California seemed like a good idea.

However, something fortuitous did happen. I met this fellow Paul, who I knew socially from my country club. He had recently left the garment business and was trying real estate as an alternative. Originally, he had some partners in his ventures but things had not worked out. We talked both our situations over and agreed to start a new real estate business together using the den of his house to launch our new enterprise: Unity Capital.

At the inception of Unity Capital, we both were in terrible financial shape although my situation was graver than Paul's. In fact, for me to get to Paul's house in Manhasset, he had to loan me $4 gas money. Obviously, our policy was to keep our expenses to a minimum. In this regard, we operated with one telephone. There were no fax machines. No cell phones. In those days, we couldn't even afford to make outgoing calls, and we never held for someone. Either the people called us back or there was no communication.

Basically, we were seeking to purchase income-producing properties and then syndicate them. We were hampered by our lack of money and had to focus on acquiring small properties. Our very first purchase was in Bronxville, New York. I had become the lead man in researching the properties we were interested in obtaining, and Paul was now the syndicator. Of course we did almost everything related to our work together. Each of us had his individual responsibilities, but we learned from each other. Paul learned about real estate from me, and I learned how important details were from a man who had been in a business where every inch of material used counted against profits. In short, Paul was a shrewd and experienced businessman and his experience complemented my own. We were virtually inseparable during these times, working hard at achieving success meant the most intimate kind of cooperation between us, and we both were well aware of that.

We made a few deals for apartment complexes. We leveraged these purchases with 20% or 30% down, and we found banks willing to work with us. We were still trying to remain in the realm of small purchases. In a range of $500,000 to $800,000. Occasionally, there was a million-dollar deal, and we would sell shares to investors at $35,000 a share. This worked well for us, and we started to improve our cash flow sufficiently to acquire a small office in Great Neck, New York. It was an office without a secretary, just an answering machine. But it was an office. At the same time, my brother Joe joined me once again. His role was to be the hands on manager of our properties. Joe was excellent at this work, and his addition to our business freed Paul and I to do what we were best at.

Our fortunes took another good turn when we acquired financial support from a legal firm. They had heard about us through a friend of mine and contacted me about the feasibility of working together on various real estate projects. Their financial access worked well for us, and we were able to assume larger and larger undertakings. Ultimately, we joined forces on four such endeavors. We were in the $2,000,000 range of acquisitions now, and the legal firm decided they could do as well on their own as with us. It was the end of our business connection with them. That was fine for us because they were receiving a nice chunk of our profits. It turned out to be fortuitous and perfect timing because a property in Toms River, New Jersey, had become available. It was a project we wanted to take on unencumbered with partners.

The Toms River property was comprised of four decaying apartment buildings built on a garbage dump. When the garbage decayed, it caused buried gas lines to be severed and some of the buildings became subject to explosions as a result. Overnight, the buildings were evacuated and boarded up. This was the condition we found them in. The bank, which owned the building, had to either tear the buildings down or find someone to rebuild and restore them. There were no takers until we came along. Because of my expertise and knowledge of architecture and construction, and Paul's abilities to raise money, this was an ideal situation for us. Therefore, we bought the property for very little money relative to its actual worth. We also bought it without using any of our own money. We arranged with the bank holding the property for a deal of no cash up front and for building loans to rebuild the complex. In fact, none of our money was invested. Eventually, a few investors did join us, but it was a coup for us.

When we began the job, we found the site was a total disaster. We had to pump chemical grout into the ground to shore up the foundations. We had to repair broken concrete and broken structures. However, by the time we finished, it became a place of beauty. All the detritus of the past was gone, replaced with what was clean and new. Along with our success in Toms River, we acquired a new team member. He was Paul's son, Robby.

22. *"Man is a computer. His brain is the processor. Alter the processor and you change the man."*

SWEET SMELL OF SUCCESS

Robby was an accountant by profession and he was just what we needed to manage all of our finances. Now, we had our team assembled, and Unity Capital was ready to move forward with a new force and dedication.

Our business exploded, and we moved to new more spacious offices in Great Neck, New York. We had in house brokers working for us looking for properties all over the country. We had an acquisitions department. We had a staff of fifteen people running the office. In short, we exceeded our wildest hopes. Our Christmas party had graduated from four people to over the one hundred that worked for us. We tried very hard to keep those one-hundred-some odd employees happy and share our success with them. They were important to us and our business, and we never forgot it.

My property in Yaphank, long held by me, became the property of Unity Capital. Paul and Robby bought in and became my partners on the parcel. We held that land while we worked on other projects, always feeling that one day it would be our ultimate achievement. In the meanwhile, we became the favorites of brokers and banks. Banks, insurance companies, and legal firms clamored to be our partners. It was a nice position to be in after all the chaos and hard times.

In the late eighties, business fell off due to new banking regulations and tax laws. The worst part of this change is that previous laws were not honored and nothing was grandfathered in under these new restrictions. This hurt the building industry gravely. Everyone suffered in the business.

Unity Capital included. We had enough experience, however, to still negotiate with our financial institutions and resolve outstanding financial matters. Our skills worked to our advantage. This happened with a prominent New York City bank. We owed them significant money, in the millions, money that they had loaned us on our Yaphank property.

We ended up settling for 10% of the debt. The way we managed this feat was by proving to the bank that the land was not worth anywhere near what it had been valued at previously. When the governor of New York State designated my land an "Economic Development Zone," I had what I needed. The designation meant there were no real estate taxes on new buildings plus a host of other advantages. I turned this positive into a negative to convince the bank that the land was worthless. It was a ploy on my part, but it worked. I called the bank officials on the phone and explained to them that the land was designated as an Economic Development Zone because it was in a blighted area. I complained, "I can't believe what is going on. I get hit from one end to the other end."

"What's the matter, Al?"

"Look, I just got killed. They made my property an Economic Development Zone for the area. These zones are only given in blighted areas to boost the economy."

"What do you mean?"

"Well, it's a Catch 22. Who's gonna want to move in that zone when they hear it is a blighted area? They screwed me! They thought they were doing me a favor, and they screwed me good."

SWEET SMELL OF SUCCESS

The bank believed my outrage to be genuine, and my land was returned to me for a minimal payment on my part.

Eventually, Paul retired and moved to Florida. Robby moved to Connecticut and manages all of Unity Capital's properties. Joe and I started a new business, but we still worked under the name "Unity Capital." The irony in all this is that the four of us were building on the original property I held in Yaphank, the very same 165 acres property that followed me from the beginning of my career to this very day, that land became worth a small fortune.

When I look back now, it is evident that those 165 acres were my life support system for almost forty years. At every turn in my business, those acres came into play one way or another and often saved me from ruin. Both individuals and banks knew about the land and treated me with an unusual deference because of its value. The Yaphank property was and is the very foundation of my success. I look back on my years of struggle and success with humility, gratitude, and appreciation of the small decisions in life that often turn into the most important choices of all.

This property presently hosts two-million-square-foot industrial park, which was sold for countless millions of dollars. In addition, I have since expanded my horizons into many other projects and a variety of different businesses. It is difficult to believe that I sit here in semi-retirement, semi only because I choose not to completely retire. I have acquired many new, young, aggressive partners all working

23. *"The heartless man said, 'You will lose much sleep if you loan money to friends and unknowns.' The caring man said, 'I will lose more if I do not.'"*

on exciting projects and businesses that range from the East coast to Florida. I remain close to many of my childhood friends, and it is quite unbelievable to me that from "the least likely to succeed." I am one who has succeeded beyond the wildest dreams of my detractors.

24. *"It is unfortunate that the wisdom of the aged cannot be transferred to the recklessness of our youth."*

Notes

Part Two

Prescription for a Successful Life

Power

Webster defines *power* as the ability to act, perform, control, and influence. Each of the words in the definition denotes a kind of action. Essentially, power is just that, an exercise to move or change the status quo. Power is a quality so potent that it can bring down nations. When we contemplate the manifestations of power in the world and in our lives, it is worthwhile to remember power is a unique human quality that resides in our brains. All of us have power. Some of us have limited powers, such as a parent over a child. Others have greater power. For example, a teacher over children or a president over a nation. Regardless of what business or profession you are in or what daily tasks you are involved with, there is a seesaw relationship to power. As a customer in a restaurant or a shopper in a retail shop, we have the perceived power. When we walk into the Motor Vehicle Bureau or deal with any other government agency, the power we have is taken from our hands and shifts to a bureaucracy. However, I do not want to imply that only government agencies abuse their power. It happens at every level in our culture. The best example of this kind of behavior is in the business world. Everyone in America is aware of the abuse of power in business now. Enron, Global Communications, and Tyco are but the tip of the iceberg in terms of the abuse of power, and let us not forget Madoff and how his abuse of power ruined the lives of many people. CEOs who make sweetheart deals for themselves and family members. CEOs who live lavishly and illegally off shareholder's money. CEOs who create incredible golden parachutes that leave them with unparalleled wealth as they leave office. Corporations that obfuscate the truth through shrewd public relations and outright lying. Ford and Firestone turned a blind eye to a bad car with bad tires. Microsoft sells software that never works and always needs upgrading, yet convincing the public this is the way things work in the computer world. Most egregious of all are the stock market manipulations of investment bankers and trading firms. The list of these perfidious and malicious behaviors is virtually inexhaustible. The victims? All of us who go out to work each day with the conviction that markets work as they are supposed to, banks are honest, corporations are responsible for their products, CEOs are decent, honest and law-abiding captains of industry, and our government will protect us with its power if there is malfeasance.

Wishful thinking and a fantasy world in view of what we see in the headlines of newspapers every day. Perceived power is more prevalent and more widely bandied about then absolute power. Many people and agencies take advantage of this silent but devastating asset. It is what intimidates people when they are approached by individuals who have acted with seeming legitimacy but have conveyed by subliminal messages what might occur without cooperation. The reason I am writing a separate chapter on power is that I want you to understand that if power is used in a positive way, accomplishments can be dramatic for a family, a business, or a political enterprise. If we can conquer our insecurities and use power to help one another, the world will be a better place to live in for all of us.

A perfect example of the correct use of power is illustrated in the public life of an old high school friend of mine, Harvey Weisenberg. Like most of us, Harvey went through school and life with his share of problems, but he worked his way through them. Today, Assemblyman Harvey Weisenberg is a shining example of what a politician can do when power is used properly. The other day at a fund-raiser, Harvey's speech centered about thanking his constituents for the power they conferred on him in order that he might serve their best interests. It was a humble speech from a humble man. But his work as an ardent advocate for the mentally ill and as an important player in the educational system of New York State speaks volumes about the man and his dedication to others. Along these same lines, Harvey is a central figure in placing lifesaving defibrillators in schools throughout the state. He has also been at the forefront of New York State's contribution to Angela's House for Disabled Children located some thirty miles away from Harvey's voting district. It's clear that Harvey has people on his mind as a wielder of power and has made himself available to anyone and everyone requiring help inside or outside his assembly district. Harvey is truly an advocate of the people. Indeed, in the last assembly election, his opponent noted, "My chances of unseating Assemblyman Weisenberg are less than favorable. He has racked up a long list of achievements in Albany. He is a friend, a good guy, and does a good job." It would serve politicians well to take note that because of Assemblyman Weisenberg's record, winning an election becomes an afterthought. The actions of a good man and servant of the people do not go unnoticed and are rewarded at the polls.

It is clear Harvey is one of the exceptions, for power is something only a few people truly understand. I certainly didn't as a young man starting out in business. I discovered the use and abuse of power is something that is thrust upon us each day in every walk of life. We are surrounded by people who revel in their power over others. Moreover, the abuse of power extends beyond the business world and encompasses our entire political, economic, and social system. The IRS, the FBI, the Congress, the President, the town supervisor, the Federal Reserve all have unique powers and the ultimate power of estoppel. Decisions by these entities can have a profound effect on the individual and the businessman. I have been a part of this system and the recipient of its awesome might. I have never seen myself as a Frank Serpico, someone who challenged the status quo. I have never been prepared to commit financial suicide to make a point. Therefore, I have worked within the system. Sometimes the law has been in my favor and a well-timed lawsuit has served my purposes. Other times it has been an inspector or some other individual that had to be dealt with. Often it has been a politician whose clout could move things along for me. I learned these lessons early in my business life.

Power is also money and resources. Making a deal with someone and completing the deal no matter how good one's attorneys are, is contingent on only one thing: who has more

---

25. *"Evil rots the core of society."*

financial and legal resources. In the final analysis it is the one with more power who prevails. It is not about who is "right." It is about who has the power. This happens all the time in the business world.

As I have noted before, perceived power often is more powerful than actual power. In my case, perceived power meant that people sometimes ascribed to me authority and control I did not actually have. I have seen this work innumerable times. Because I was friendly with many people in high places, people approached me with requests that required political influence. On the other hand, this perception of my power via my friends let me sail through many situations because the people I dealt with knew my connections.

The core of my philosophy in regard to the use and abuse of power is something my mother told me many years ago. She said I would face many difficult times in life and sometimes I would do the wrong thing in relation to my power. The way to face my mistakes was to stand up to them like a man, and I would be just fine. She also said never give in when I was right in the face of arbitrary power no matter how difficult the road. I took her advice to heart in dealing with the many agencies and individuals who had the power to affect my business and it has served me well.

26. *"The eye cannot see what the heart feels."*

Notes

Prescription for a Successful Life

So you think we are different? How do we differ? By our coloring? By our emotions? By our organs? No. What is different is the way we live. Our lifestyles encompass so much diversity; it is hard to believe that we share the same earth. I have read about the way you live. I have heard about the way you live, and I have even seen the way you live, but make no mistake about it, I do not understand your way of life much more than you understand mine. If you do not have my good fortune, try to imagine coming home to a quiet and peaceful neighborhood. A home that is neat and clean. A refrigerator that is full of food and cabinets stuffed with goodies? Rooms that are individually heated in the winter and cooled in the summer, rooms having a Wii and Xbox flat screen TVs DVRs or Blu-ray discs laptops computers and iPads all synced up with our iPhones to go. Closets filled with clothes for countless special occasions. Shelves filled with games, toys, books, art supplies, and just about any interest or hobby and, in some cases, rooms with their own bathrooms. If you are a teen, can you imagine borrowing your dad's car or in most cases taking your own? Can you imagine being handed a hundred-dollar bill from your parents for a night on the town with your Friends or taking a weekend trip to your home in the mountains? How about getting on an airplane and flying to an exotic island with tantalizing hotels, romantic sunsets, and ocean sounds to help mellow the mind and body? Can you imagine having family contacts in high and important places willing to offer their help? Can you imagine a choice of what schools to go to or what career to pursue in life? Can you imagine opportunities limited only by your own imagination and individual drive? Can you imagine all of that?

I cannot imagine not having those things any more than I can imagine walking through drug infested streets lined with hookers, users, pushers, killers, and fearing every step might be my last. I can't imagine fearing for my life merely by walking through the hallways to my apartment. I cannot imagine entering my apartment with no feeling of relief from the elements. I cannot imagine space being shared by a family needing three times the area at their disposal. Nor can I imagine rooms without beds and rooms often shared with rodents and other unwelcome guests. I can't imagine a life where televisions, radios, DVRs, and cell phones are alien and where refrigerators wait to be filled or cabinets to be filled with treats. I cannot imagine a world where bathrooms, even if in working order, are so substandard that use of them is revolting. I can't imagine a life where to achieve transport one must hop onto the back of a moving bus or be pulled on a skateboard by a truck through dangerous streets or steal into a subway for an illegal ride. I can't imagine a world where having a date means hanging with the gang. I can't conceive of a world where the closest one comes to the sound of the ocean is a leaky pipe. I cannot imagine not being free to even have the luxury to plan for tomorrow when today is unresolved.

I can't imagine attending a school where the most important tool to learn is self-defense and where students run corridors and classrooms by gang rule, a place where the teachers are powerless, principals are figureheads, superintendents are spineless, education is a nonexistent, and society is the enemy. I cannot imagine not having hope for the future, not being able to dream, to not sharing exactly what the boy around the corner has.

Why are there such differences in the human experience? Why do these inconsistencies exist? It is not because of color, nor race, nor religion, but because all mankind possesses the singular gift that makes us superior to our surroundings: a brain…an organ so powerful that it controls every one of the millions of things happening in the body at one time while it also preserves the ability for man to think independently. One could theorize that this wonderful ability to expand human powers and imagination would bring a melting pot of opportunities for all mankind. Why isn't that the case? What has gone wrong? The brain has gone wrong. For example, we have all been in parking lots crowded with white cars, black cars, red cars, and yellow cars. These cars have many different home environments that distinguish them from one other. Some are from the posh areas, others from the slums. Some are clean. Well cared for and fed the proper ingredients for a long life while others are ill-treated and shown little love. These cars, with all their shades of difference, from geographic location to ornamentation, to color, converge in this massive parking lot. Not one of them would ever attempt to invade the privacy of his fellow car. However, place a brain in the control box a human being behind the wheel, and this heretofore peace-loving dinosaur, submitting to its master's travel needs, can become a ferocious animal, a potential threat to the life of almost everything in its path including the friendly car that was previously by its side. Now that peaceful and respectful existence has been marred by the injection of a brain, and it is that brain, which creates what is referred to today as "road rage." The injection of a brain gone awry in this scenario points out its potential destructive energy and suggests that for people to succeed, programming the brain in a positive direction is the best answer to the challenge of life.

27. *"Another man's success is only an image that reality can shatter."*

Notes

Control Your Future

I am a strong believer in molding your destiny with every decision you make. My theory has always been to thank God for all the good deals and understand that there are always some bad deals in life. That premise has brought me to the spot where I am today. And where I am today is an enviable and very satisfying personal, economic, and social position. I have never regretted any deal I created, even the major losers. My philosophy has been to never look back and keep going forward. I have traveled that road and all the twists and turns of choice without second-guessing myself or using twenty-twenty hindsight. If the energy most of us waste agonizing over the past could be channeled toward the future, the results and the rewards would be surprising. We must learn how to let go of what has happened in the past, and use those experiences to improve our future. We can't worry about a past that has already happened or about the future that has not occurred.

We have all heard the phrase "failure breeds success." Failure gives us the experience, the knowledge, the foundation for wisdom, and the stepping-stone for achievement. The experiences of the past should be used as a learning experience to replace negative thoughts with an abundance of positive energy. If you understand this theory, you can and will conclude that there is no such thing as failure just a temporary delay while preparing and learning for future growth.

Life is a perception; our achievements and desires are the product of our imagination. Thus, only the depth of our ability to imagine limits our goals. There is nothing we use, nothing we read, nothing man made that has not been an image in someone's mind before it was born, whether it is a paper clip or a computer.

It has been said, "You are here by the road you have traveled." These words have much weight. We all look at the same objects but see them differently. Listening to two individuals describe a book, a painting, or a movie could leave a third person totally confused and with an entirely different perspective. Therefore, it can then be concluded that what is "real" is the consequence of one's perception or imagination. Since that is case, and since our imagination is not "real," nothing is real. Reality is simply how we perceive it. Perception is reality; since we control perception, we control reality and, thus, our future.

I believe in destiny, but I am not a fatalist. Some believe their lives are prearranged and their future already written. I believe we determine our own destiny. People need to be awakened and sensitized enough to realize that we are masters of our own fate. Our destiny follows our belief in who we are. Once this belief is cemented in our minds, unless changed, it becomes our life, good or bad.

28. *"The ability to achieve is as limitless as your ability to imagine."*

Notes

Imagery

We are what we think we are. Unfortunately, many of us do not have positive thoughts about ourselves, and it is that negativity that prevents most of us from achieving. For example, in the world of sports, imagery is most important. The principal called cyber vision is common practice in teaching an athlete proper movements. If one picks up a golf club, having never played or watched someone play, his attempt at hitting the ball can be disastrous. On the other hand, someone who from time to time has watched a pro swinging at the ball would try to mimic the motion using imagery. Cyber vision is the use of imagery to perfect a mental image so your brain can mimic any athletic movement to fit your physical capabilities.

Choose a sport that interests you, be it golf, skiing, or any sport that requires physical movements. Convince yourself of one thing: if your brain can imagine the proper movement, it will transfer that image to your physical movement. So the better the image is and the more we believe in the image, the better the physical results. After all, body parts are only doing with the brain tells them to do.

This technique extends to prayer. Praying is another form of imagery, and since what we are asking for is not yet

IMAGERY

a reality, one can focus on the police and strive to make it a reality.

Another aspect of imagery involves sex. Unlike fear, which is either instinctual or learned, we are all born with the ability and biological makeup to experience sex. All sexual acts start with the brain and an image. If the mind likes what it is seeing, thinking, feeling, or dreaming, sexual feelings intensify. If the mind is distracted, irritated, or discouraged, sexual feelings diminish. Hence, boredom, problems in a relationship, or stress will impede the ability to react sexually.[29]

There isn't a therapist worth his degree who wouldn't agree that sex often is a mental state. While sex between two people may be described as a physical attraction, a chemical reaction, or a bonding, most often it all starts with a mental image. Many men suffering from impotence have mental, not physical, problems. Impotence can come from various forms of negativity: sexual rejection, spousal abuse, poor self-image, boredom, or a self-proclaimed prophecy that age has taken its toll. I am sure you have heard men say, "I think about it in my head, but can't transform it to other parts of my body," or "At my age I feel like a dog chasing cars." When in a conscious state, these men are unable to have an erection; but when sleeping, they have no problems attaining an erection because the mind is able to function unencumbered. Whatever suppressed mental problems they have during consciousness are nonexistent in sleep, and all that is left for a therapist to change are the negative images that occur in a conscious state. "The weight of true love can tip the scales of justice."

29. *"When the heart is empty, we are alone."*

Similarly, positive thinking and proper mental imaging can cure whatever category of problems you have. Working with a therapist is an important approach. However, if you cannot change your mental imaging into strong positive thoughts, no one can help. For example, couples who practice imagery and press their imaginations to the outer limits enjoy a long, fruitful, and exciting sex life. Sensuality and sexuality are states of mind. If sex were merely mechanical or physical and not mental, we would be attracted to everyone. Reading about the power of the brain, agreeing and understanding the verbiage, is not the same as believing and being totally convinced and committed to the absolute fact that we will have success in our lives if we use our brainpower and positive imagery in everything we do every day.

We have all witnessed sporting events that have produced mammoth upsets. Teams and individuals have reached goals never thought possible. On any given day, for whatever reason, the underdog has his brain in the right place. The win is a dream (an image), but the desire and the image are so strong that the brain reacts to the challenge and becomes an ally too powerful for any opponent. This phenomenon was evident in the 1980 Winter Olympics when the United States hockey team, tremendous underdogs, not only made it to the finals but also beat the heretofore never defeated Russians. This was not luck. It was an image so strong that it became a reality.

A sculptor selects a piece of rock or a piece of wood, studies it, closes his eyes, and eventually sees a shape within the object. After that image is created and is fixed in his brain, all that is left is to chisel away at the excess material until the perceived image is transformed from the brain to the object. The wood or stone has become, actualized by someone's imagination. Who knows what another sculptor would have seen in the same original material. Using the same process as the sculptor, imaging, and then chipping away at the excess to create an object of art is also a very productive way to shape our bodies. How many people do you know that go on diets? Ask any of these people what their goal is. The most likely answer is, "I would like to lose ten, twenty, or whatever pounds." That answer invariably leads to failure along with an ongoing saga of various diets, one worse than the other. These people continue to fail, and each time they do so, and in their quest for weight loss they do untold damage to their bodies. Obviously, diets do not work alone. Physical exercise must also be included, but most importantly a mental image of what you want your body to look like must exist. Go to any gym in the country and the one thing you see more than anything else is mirrors, mirrors, and more mirrors. This is because mirrors allow people to look at and mentally focus on the particular body part being worked on. Once the brain sees the muscle, it can focus, and only through this mental focusing, can muscle develop.

There are no body builders you see that do not continuously set a mental image of what they want to look like. Likewise, a mental image is the key to financial success. People who achieve financial success do so because they have strong desires to have the power and the luxury success

---

30. *"To live only in the world and not the imagination is to waste God's gift to us."*

brings. No successful person in business reaches his goals without countless hours of mental imaging. Mega complexes have been built, countless products have been produced, astonishing inventions enter our society every day and start-up corporations make mammoth financial breakthroughs, all through the power of the brain and its ability to imagine. People who do not dream of financial success and the benefits it affords can never reach it and, if by chance they do, in most cases will lose what they have. Studies done on people who have become enriched on lottery winnings show a significant number of these individuals have lost their fortunes, mainly because their brains were not programmed to accommodate their new wealth. Therefore, a person who imagines his climb to personal wealth every day has the opportunity to grow into the situation. On the other hand, someone who has an overnight win is thrown into a situation he may have wished for. Thus, he is ill prepared to deal with his new wealth because he does not truly believe such a circumstance can occur. Remember, I said wanting it and believing it are two different things. You can want and you can wish, but if you truly do not believe in most cases, you are doomed for failure.

Imagery is a personal thing. We all do it many more times a day than we realize. Its most simplistic use is when we are yearning for a particular dinner. The image of that meal is on our mind; sometimes so strong we can almost taste it. The imaging process will vary according to individual personalities. I suggest that you start the process while in bed, and before sleep, lying on your back, totally relaxed, allow your mind to carry your body to a foreign but comfortable and exotic place. While in this state of total relaxation, begin

IMAGERY

forming the images of your most desired wishes. Actually, visualize the result. The conclusion actually happening. Most important, however, is affirmation. Affirmation, simply put, in this case means agreeing with one's inner self that indeed you have reached your desired images. For example, assume you have been exercising and adhering to proper dietary meals. Begin imagining your body perfectly shaped and affirming that indeed. "I do look wonderful. My body looks exactly the way I want it to look. I have achieved my lifelong goal, etc., etc." The same process should be used to cure illness. Imagine a healthy body. One operating in perfect harmony, feeling young and strong. Keep affirming the result as you imagine it. Remember, that our destiny is our belief in ourselves.

I taught this method to one of my daughters. She's afraid of heights and was very uncomfortable skiing. For several nights, I went through imagery sessions, first showing her professional skiers and pointing out their form. I then told her to close her eyes and picture her head on their bodies; and over the next few weeks, there was a major improvement in her ability to ski and her fear was conquered on the mountain.

31. "Stupidity is most dangerous when we will not admit to it."

Notes

The Brain: Conscious, Subconscious

At all times we must keep in mind that the only thinking and behavior-controlling organ we have in our bodies is our brain. It controls everything we do physically and psychologically. One theory of human behavior suggests we have a voluntary (conscious) and involuntary (subconscious) mind. In this model, the subconscious mind operates without conscious control and has an effect on our behavior. Processes like the circulation of the blood, the growth of our cells, and the total operation of all our organs are functions of our brain stem, the primitive element in the conventional three-part model of the brain. The cerebrum and cerebellum deal with our behaviors and our cognitive abilities and what might be termed our "psychology." We are all pre-programmed for our conscious behaviors. Thus, a woman is programmed to be more maternal than men are. They bear and raise children. A man is programmed to be more protective, to be the hunter-gatherer. This programming resides somewhere in our subconscious mind. It is a well-known fact that when a baby cries during the night hours they are more likely to be heard by the mother whereas noise from an intrusion will in most cases awaken the man. The subconscious mind is always at work, even when we sleep. Scientists have been studying brain growth in the fetus and research has demonstrated that sensitivity, curiosity, and emotions are definitely present. This is another example of the subconscious mind at work even before birth.

Dreams are another example of the subconscious mind at work. Researchers agree that with proper guidance one can learn to program dreams. Dreams can give us an insight to our inner selves, help solve life's problems, increase our creativity, and help with all kinds of health problems. Dreams reveal the subconscious mind; they are our third eye with an x-ray vision of our inner self. Learning to interpret, induce, or remember a dream is the subject of many books. I strongly suggest you acquire such books. Being able to work with your dreams and learning to unleash your subconscious mind will help change your life forever. The voluntary or conscious mind operates on command. It performs all the daily functions we experience. It is the voluntary mind that takes a shower, eats our breakfast, and gets dressed and all other "thinking" functions that take place in our life.

Strangely enough, we can control our subconscious mind or involuntary actions by making them part of the conscious, or voluntary, mind. We have often seen people walk on fire, glass, and perform other astonishing acts. Most of us are quick to conclude that there is some magic trickery occurring. The truth is that these people have taken control of their involuntary mind with whatever method they have learned to use; in the case of walking on fire, having trained the brain not to feel the heat, and when walking on glass, having trained the brain to not only control pain but the flow of blood. Doubt it? Well then, let's take an example we can all

THE BRAIN: CONSCIOUS, SUBCONSCIOUS

relate to. We all agree that circulation of the blood, breathing, and blinking is a part of our involuntary system. The brain performs all three examples without us being aware of the process, similar to all of the other operations of our organs. To illustrate the point, however, concentrate on your breathing and your blinking. Surprise, it's easy to control each of them. We can stop breathing or take many quick breaths, or we can blink or not blink. More challenging, perhaps, might be controlling the flow of our blood, something we have not been trained to do. Interestingly enough though, the right word at the right time will make most of us blush. Blushing is caused by an increase in blood flow to a given area.

All it takes is a simple word or situation to stimulate the flow of blood, and there is an involuntary reaction. It can, therefore, be assumed that with the proper training, it might be possible the brain can control almost any part of our involuntary system, even the chain of events that produces blushing.

Controlling our involuntary system is not a goal that most of us aspire to. However, the belief that our mind is strong enough and that we can achieve such control, if properly trained, will lead us to success in areas of personal growth and to a height of achievement previously unattainable.

As a matter of fact, it is important to know that most of these involuntary actions are essential to life. Pain, for example, is a beacon to locate and act upon a problem that would otherwise go untreated. Fear, another involuntary action, also sends out important signals. Fear, like pain, is a warning sign that should not be ignored. Indeed, the brain stores memories of both pain and pleasure. If we did not remember things we liked or experiences of danger, we couldn't repeat the pleasure or protect against the dangers; this would make survival unlikely. The subconscious mind will send out signals when a situation occurs that the conscious mind should be aware of. Fear will manifest itself in many forms: the fear of taking a test, the fear of performing to an audience, or the fear of bodily harm. Regardless of the reason, the feeling is usually the same with the possible difference of the fear for one's life, which would be more intense.

Fear, like pain, can be our friend. Past experiences gathered by our subconscious minds will send out signals that make us focus on a situation. Most of us do not use this opportunity properly. We waste our energy focusing on the negative, thereby reaffirming the fear and making it worse. This action produces more negative energy and impedes the brain from acting or functioning properly. That negative energy must be redirected to positive thoughts. Whether it is fear from testing, public performance, bodily harm, or any other form fear might take, your conscious mind must think positive thoughts. For example, fill your mind with positives like, "I'm well prepared for this exam," or "I have studied well." The same goes for public speaking or bodily confrontation. As we constantly push our conscious mind to think positively, two major things occur. First, we are reprogramming the negative energy to positive energy, leading to more productive results and, in time, reducing fear. Secondly, if we are feeding our minds with positive thoughts, one no longer has the time to think negatively. This cuts off a negative flow of energy to your brain. As a result, the brain is being fed positive thoughts to overcome the previously implanted negativity. The outcome is success in better controlling and understanding our fears.

Remember that fear comes from wisdom and wisdom comes from life's experiences. While there is some evidence we are born with the three primary emotions of fear, anger, and love in place, we develop each quite rapidly. A negative experience allowed to fester in one's mind will manifest itself as fear when the same situation arises again in the future. Fear is a signal that we are about to embark upon a situation that needs our attention. Fear is a friend. It is a warning similar to the warning given by the beacon of pain. In both situations, we are being alerted by our subconscious mind. It's how the mind handles the signal that will determine the output. Facial expressions are another example of the body and mind connection through the subconscious mind. Facial expressions can communicate emotions in a split second. If trained to read these expressions, one can know what the subconscious mind is saying. The ability to read one's subconscious mind will always reveal the truth. Infants communicate most emotions with facial expressions: anger, fear, sadness, surprise, and happiness. All these are also very detectable in adult facial expressions. Thus, smiling is another representation of our conscious and subconscious minds at work. We are preconditioned to know that when we smile we are in a "happy" mood. The act can be a conscious one, but the meaning is definitely subconscious. Try this: think of something very sad and ponder the thought as though it

---

32. *"Friendship is based on a perception of what is; only in need is the true measure of friendship known."*

is a reality for a few moments. Now, place a smile on your face and think of the same unpleasant situation. Surprise you can't think bad things when there is a smile on your face. The subconscious mind has been preconditioned to believe that a smile means to be happy, and it is so ingrained that as soon as the smile appears. The mood changes, which means happiness is a choice we can all consciously make.

Similarly, people hear music and the brain immediately sends signals of an emotional encounter. Music strikes a chord in the brain. Merely changing the beat, the tone, or the words can create moods. The reaction is controlled by our subconscious mind. Consider reflexology for a moment. Reflexology is a therapy in which pressure is applied to reflex points, on the hands, feet, and ears. The theory is that the body is divided into ten zones running from each toe to the brain then to the fingers. Thus, there are five zones on each side. The proper manipulation of one of these zones will send a signal to the brain and bring a therapeutic effect to the area affected by pain. This method of healing, dating back to the ancient Egyptian and Chinese cultures is another example of subconscious brainpower being used to cure and/or prevent illness. Remember, as the body heals itself from a surface wound, such as a cut, it draws upon its subconscious and innate brainpowers to send the signal, which knits together tissue in order for the body to act upon its natural healing abilities. Thus, to achieve and maintain good health, one must adopt a nutritious diet. A regular exercise program, a

---

33. *"Love scorned is attacked by ego and emotion, and both have no brain."*

positive mental outlook, and some control of the interaction of our conscious and subconscious mind.

Emotional pain is a combination of the conscious and subconscious mind. The experience is registered in the conscious mind, but the reaction comes from the subconscious mind. For emotional pain to be truly damaging often there has to be intent. When you feel hurt by others actions, first and foremost one must ask was it the intent to hurt, or was it just my perception or misinterpretation of what was intended? Too many times, relationships suffer because of misinterpretations and poor communication. Even when an emotional wound is the intention, for it to be damaging someone whose opinion you respect and admire must administer it. Someone of lesser stature or whose opinion you do not respect should not have the ability to inflict emotional pain. In order for a person to hurt you, he must be held in high esteem in relation to the subject matter being discussed. A person you do not hold in high regard or do not respect should not have the power to hurt you.

One must not waste time loving material items that cannot love back. Not that materialism is bad; it is just incapable of satisfying our innate need for love. Indeed, in many cases we confuse true emotional love with our desire for material gain. This leads us to an emotional dissatisfaction that manifests itself in a form of frustration. Love is an emotion; it is a need that must be satisfied by both giving and receiving. Love is a combination of the conscious and subconscious

---

34. *"If God created what man can overcome, can God be among the living?"*

mind working in harmony. Love encompasses physical love, and physical love is a perfect example of the pleasures that can be derived when the conscious and subconscious mind are in harmony, and it is sad that this most pleasurable life-affirming act is today tainted with fear, abuse, and general negativity. Finally, we must not confuse love with the need to always obey. We may love our spouses, our parents, our bosses, but we do not always have to agree with or accept their opinions.

Notes

Preconditioning

Aging is a fascinating process. Just what our current age is, is a question many of us stop answering as life progresses. Nonetheless, aging and its ramifications is a process we are well aware of from our childhood. If we had been born in the early 1700s, we might be programmed to believe that twenty-five is old. Clearly, as the centuries have passed, what was considered old has changed. In the year 2000, eighty was considered old, and now more people are living to be 100, and soon that will be the norm. This sequence is an example of preconditioning.

Preconditioning is what we as a society suffer from. Have you ever seen an elephant on display at a fair chained by one leg to a meek post in the ground? A tug on the chain with only a fraction of the elephant's strength would set it free to escape. However, when the elephant is younger, as part of its training, the same chain is attached to a massive concrete anchor. The young, untrained, and by nature wild beast fights ferociously to break loose. After whatever time it takes, the elephant finally acquiesces to the fact that it cannot set itself free. Consequently, it stops trying. Now preconditioned, when the same chain is placed on the elephant's leg but tethered to a less sturdy anchor, the elephant does not even try to escape.

PRECONDITIONING

Although you and I know all the elephant has to do is use a minimum of its strength to break free, the elephant does not. Some humans view this elephant as stupid. Can't it at least try to free itself? Well, stupid as the elephant may be, we are not too far behind. Most adults are so preconditioned in so many areas of life that the sum total of what you are. How you think, react, and in general, the life you lead is basically preconditioned. We look at others in awe relative to some behaviors and wonder why they can't see things the way we do—preconditioning just like the elephant.

However, there are some people just as there are some elephants freeing themselves of this preconditioning. People who break away and begin to rethink their preconditioning are the ones who take control of their lives and travel in new directions. Unfortunately, it is not always a direction that society values. For example, dictators and tyrants have this quality. How we think about the aging process is not dissimilar to the trained elephant's experience. We are conditioned to believe that age is synonymous with deterioration. To a degree age is, but the guidelines we use are erroneous. Time, as we know, has nothing or little to do with aging. Preconceived beliefs condition our brains into accepting an aging schedule. How many times have we heard, "I'm getting so old? I'm too old to do that." Time goes too fast. The best example of this is when the actuaries of the world give us the average age of death for a man or woman and how it changes from state to state and country to country. Once these statistics are

35. *"Listening to the problems of others trivializes our own but rarely helps to change or comfort us."*

posted, we begin to program our brains to those numbers. When we approach that mathematical age limit, we then believe we are getting older, and because of that belief, it then becomes a self-fulfilling prophecy. Self-fulfilling prophecies are common-day occurrences. In the past, doctors of family members never divulged the inevitable result of a terminal illness to a patient. Compare that style of medicine to the present-day practice of telling all. I believe the patients with no knowledge of certain death have lived longer because they do not focus on the negative. Their brain has not been preoccupied with dying; consequently, they live longer in many cases.

Age is only a word; years and time are only reference points, made up by man for purposes of communication. If a year were twenty-four months, you would be half your present age, or if a year were six months, you would be twice as old.

If you can believe that time has no meaning since it is man-made, then age has no bearing or effect on our lives other than those preconceived thoughts ingrained in our subconscious mind that must be changed. Of course, we do things to shorten our own life span and, consequently, help toward creating a self-fulfilling prophecy. Time and age mean nothing, and with a strong belief in that fact, we can have a direct effect on the aging process. However, without the proper care of our bodies, diet and exercise, looking and acting youthful, we contribute to our own aging process. We too are mechanical devices that if not cared for properly, if not fed the proper ingredients, will fail before their time.

36. *"One's desires cannot come before one's needs."*

PRECONDITIONING

There is no magic formula, no pill to take, no easy way out. In order to live an extended healthy existence, look and feel young, one must combine a positive mental image along with proper physical and nutritional habits. Nothing else works.

Notes

Healing

Healing is a process that takes place through the subconscious mind. The brain is constantly sending waves to body wounds, and the healing process is taking place even as we sleep. The most obvious example of this process is the surface wound that grows a scab over a few days. Eventually, the damaged area is returned to its normal state. If you can imagine your affected area totally cured, normal and healthy, those are the waves the brain will project. After all, your brain created the image.

A major link between the mind and healing is faith. In order to have faith, we must have desire, belief, and expectations (an image showing the result, the goal). Belief is what turns the brain on and into a powerful source of healing power. Belief also gives us a destination a desired result. With that desired result, the brain can now focus and work toward the healing process it visualizes. Remember the mind controls. Now, all we have to do is control the mind, and we can do this if we have a strong belief in the result. Stress is a major cause of illness. It weakens the immune system. We are all programmed for stress and consequently our bodies react. Unpleasant situations, which reoccur, attack our nervous system and, if prolonged, will make us ill.

Our beliefs or expectations can produce negative or positive results. Expectations, whether negative or positive, are reinforced by visualization and imagination. As previously discussed, a strong visualization and imagination are what make things happen: positive or negative. To understand the power of the brain, consider hypnotism. When placed under this influence, we have seen people do extraordinary things. This is the process of someone else taking control of our subconscious brain, and the brain then reacting to alien commands. Thus, under the influence of hypnosis, we can control pain; change bad habits, and create a feeling of euphoria.

There are many methods used to control the functions of the brain. It is important to understand that brainpower is not a new theory and research consistently seeks to reveal new truths. Scientists realize that understanding and being able to change brainpower can unleash a whole new world of healing.

Notes

The Computer

Our brain, approximately three pounds in weight, is undergoing intensive studies by scientists. With the use of man's newly developed toy, the computer, researchers are learning things about the brain and its many different functions and capabilities that were previously unknown. Computers have existed in our society for many years but lacked the sophistication and versatility they now possess. The capabilities of today's computers were unimaginable to the masses twenty-five years ago. However, people like Bill Gates, Steven Jobs, and Steven Wosniak had an image and a belief strong enough to fulfill a dream. That dream became today's computer. Initially, the government was the backbone of computer use. The Pentagon and researchers needed a way to communicate that had a utility not found in telephones. Businesses soon joined the digital parade for they discovered keeping of inventories, receivables, payables, and other laborious chores were less labor intensive as a result of computers. They also discovered added efficiency in this new technology. The industry actuated a most sophisticated

37. *"Love comes in many packages. It's the wrapping that attracts but the content that is meaningful."*

and imaginative group of mathematicians, scientists, and entrepreneurs. They were more aggressive regarding the capabilities of these computers. As this brain developed, it produced the most revolutionary, the most sophisticated and unknown to them. Potentially, the most dangerous piece of machinery ever conceived.

As the computer industry grows, I predict that its potential ability and varied capabilities will without doubt, far exceed the destructive capabilities of the atomic bomb. Every household item imported into the US could be equipped with a computer chip. This chip, when activated by a signal sent from a main station, could be programmed to explode; hence, cyber war is just one of the many potential evils of computers, but the computer phenomenon is in its infancy.

What it can do and will be able to do in the future is beyond most of our expectations. Remember that its limitations are limited only by the imagination of those working on its future. Science has discovered that only 10% of our brain is being used. Imagine if we could add just 2 to 3% more, not to mention 20, 30, or even 50% increase.

These goals are attainable as we gain more understanding of the intricacies and functions of the brain through the use of computers. The technology of the future is limitless. The world will change so drastically in such geometric proportions that very few of us are even able to comprehend an everyday lifestyle.

The unimaginable, inconceivable of today will be the commonplace of tomorrow. There is one major underlying

38. *"Program your processor with positive power and see the results."*

factor that makes the computer phenomenon different than any other in our world. Heretofore, we have had innumerable new industries develop, such as radio, television, personal communications, etc. However advanced these industries have become, they never have had the all-embracing quality of the computer. Because the computer has attracted more brains nationwide than any current industry, tremendous brainpower has been focused toward the growth of the computer. People are attracted to the industry. More users go online every day. More businesses rely on computers and virtually every individual relies on a computer many more times than he realizes. From simple adding machines, to desktop powerhouses, the industry shows a growth pattern equal to none.

Only the power of the microprocessor limits small computers and large computers, and the brain programmed to control it. Suffice to say that with the attraction of such huge quantities of people into the computer world makes the future capabilities of computers limitless. Therefore, hold on and strap yourself in for an experience and changing world that only is limited by man's ability to imagine.

39. *"To love is to enjoy the pleasures of one another."*

Notes

The Brain: A Microprocessor

In thinking about computers, keep one fact in mind at all times: the output is only as good as the input. If incorrect information is fed into the computer, the like will be forthcoming and vice versa. If the information coming out is distasteful, objectionable, or plain wrong, man will reprogram the microprocessor, and this previously monstrous unfriendly machine can become your best friend and help guide you through many of life's experiences. A computer consists of a microprocessor, a central processing unit. This is its brain. There are also multitudes of circuit boards each distributing directions for sound, video, and telephony. Ultimately, all the desired information is fed to a monitor screen. All of these hundreds of different parts operated by the CPU and are held together by a skin, the box. Each box is different in size, color, or shape and each computer has different data than its neighbor. Sound familiar? Well, sorry folks, science cloned a sheep and President Clinton was worried that this breakthrough would lead to cloning people. People are similar to clones. People are also like computers. Make no mistake about it; each and every one of us is fed information from his surroundings. We are programmed from birth to death. It is that programming that makes us all different.

THE BRAIN: A MICROPROCESSOR

Many view the programming we receive from birth to age ten as the main element in what shapes our development, from killer to entrepreneur. From the day we are born, other brains are programming our brain, until we have stored in our database the information they wish to integrate. No one is born with the feeling of hate. An individual must be taught to function that way in a society. The emotion just depends on who it is doing the programming. That, as much as anything, determines what the results will be. As previously discussed, our surroundings, and the people who play an important part in our lives precondition us. We are little robots running around mimicking our programmers who themselves have been programmed by others. Our CPU, the brain, feeds information to our central system circuits and circuit boards, which in turn operate the different parts of our body. A skin, the case protects all of our organs and systems, differs infinitely in size, shape, color, and information. If we don't program our brains properly to deal with these human variations, then God help us.

That is the difference between a computer and human beings. We have the ability to program ourselves. If we step back and take a good look, we have the power to reprogram, think positively and advance ourselves, but only after overcoming the negativity fed to us by other people, most of whom we don't want to be like anyway, most of whom we don't respect, and most of whom we want to be better than. Why listen to someone who gives us advice that we do

---

40. *"Believe in what you see, but what you see is an image of what you believe."*

not relate to? If we are seeking someone's advice on starting a business and we listen to someone who has been in the work force for twenty-five years but has never been a boss, the wrong brain is programming us. Only seek information from someone we respect and someone we want to emulate. Never listen to anyone who has not achieved a position in life we admire.

Remember that loving someone has nothing to do with taking or not taking his or her advice. Finding a mentor can be one of the best things to happen to a career. A mentor is a wise and trusted counselor who has already achieved success in your chosen field. He has failed the requisite number of times and has risen again and again. He has weathered all the pitfalls and is prepared to pass that wisdom to others. It took this successful person twenty to thirty years to learn the secret of success.

Why not take advantage of his valuable history, talent, and knowledge to cut years off that process for you? Loving someone and respecting that person's position in life are two different things. Only seek information from someone you respect and hope to emulate. Never listen to someone who has not achieved a position you do not admire. Remember loving someone has nothing to do with taking or not taking his or her advice. There is no room in your life for negativity. If you are the average person, you have already had enough negativity. If you program yourself, program for the positive and not the negative.

41. *"We are all born with love; we learn about evil."*

Notes

Labeling

When discussing the power of the brain, there are two labels commonly used by our educators that, in my opinion, have never been explained properly? Learning disabled (LD) and IQ are two of the terms used to label and measure the ability of people, mainly children. I am not a doctor, a psychiatrist, or an educator, just an ordinary layman who is LD and challenges these psychometricians and condemns them for not making it crystal clear in ordinary language what these terms really mean.

There was a time when a student who was labeled LD had a stigma attached to him. The stigma was due to the ignorance of most people who did not understand the true meaning of LD. Unfortunately, even some educators fell into this category. People so stigmatized by LD were sometimes thought of as stupid, backward, and unable to learn. Consequently, they had little or no chance to achieve. That is also true today to some extent. However, the truth is so contrary to this common belief that professionals and others who subscribe to this notion should understand that such labeling can result in giving LD children a damaging self-image, thus adding to their handicap and impeding their growth.

LABELING

LD merely means the inability to learn or comprehend as quickly as others do in the routine tasks of school. The operative phrase is "as quickly." I did not say the inability to learn or comprehend. The key words here are "as quickly" or "as easily" to learn as others. I am LD, and so are my two daughters, one of whom graduated high school valedictorian with a four-year scholarship to college. The other completed her master's degree in education.

As I have noted, my elementary and high school days were disastrous. In the 1940s and 1950s, no one knew the term LD, and consequently, my IQ scores were below normal (a subject we will consider next). I could not read until I was thirteen, and I could not comprehend simple math. The labels I carried from class to class, from year to year, teacher to teacher, to principal were "stupid," "low IQ," "no ability to learn." The word was, "Just graduate him and send him out to pasture."

College was more than difficult for me. It was a constant struggle to survive and carrying the thought of being someone with a low IQ and LD did not help. However, I never let go of that dream that image I created. Once at college, I was having a problem learning a complicated mathematical formula. This formula was the key to designing and figuring the sizes of structural steel to be used in buildings. A friend who learned the equation and all its derivatives in no time spent hours explaining it to me. When I finally understood and learned the principle, some days later an amazing thing

---

42. *"Praying is a form of imagery since what we are asking for is not yet attained."*

happened that changed my life forever. Once I had learned and understood the formula. I began to use it in ways that most never thought of. My brain was now able to dissect and analyze this formula far better than most students, including the one who taught it to me. I didn't understand what was happening, but I began to build my confidence and develop an attitude so positive that all I could think of. All I could imagine was walking up and getting my degree in architecture. It was a dream I accomplished. Imagery surely did it for me.

It was not until I had children of school age that I first heard the term LD. It was not until then that I realized what I had suffered from. I always teased my children by saying, "That was my gift to you." Recognizing that LD is what I was and what I am, I was able to help them through the problem and cope with the issues of being learning disabled. It was then that I was able to reflect on my college days and more particularly my struggle to learn. It also was clear to me that my abilities exceeded that of many of my peers and that the labels "LD" and "low IQ" were poor predictors of my human potential.

What we must understand is that LD is not anything more than the inability to grasp things quickly and has nothing to do with intelligence or achievement, and while we are beating up on terms and those who introduce them to our lexicon, let's discuss IQ. One has only to know that H. H. Goddard, who applied the test to immigrants coming to America, popularized IQ in the United States. Goddard and his test have about as much validity as phrenology. Robert Yerkes didn't do much better with his test of millions of soldiers in World War I. in fact, there has never been a

LABELING

comprehensive definition of IQ, and there is no IQ that truly measures all the diverse intelligences a human being might possess.

Notwithstanding the above, some professional educators and social scientists have tried to define IQ as the ability to reason verbally and mathematically. Educators often relate this talent to the ability to learn and indirectly the ability to be successful academically. However, the method used for this measurement is absurd almost laughable, but the real damage is in the potentially damaging results it produces. When I was in school, Stanford-Benet testing was administered during our formative years. The finished exam was graded, and the result came back with a number: 60, 90, and 125, etc., which then was compared to a normed number. If the result was below average, then an individual was marked for life as an intellectual misfit. Conversely, if a test taker did well, he was cloaked with superlatives.

Some teachers treated students with high or low scores accordingly. Neither group was taught how to deal with its results. Even worse than that, the result was fallacious and extremely narrow-minded. If there was any correlation between IQ scores and intelligence, it was so badly handled and misunderstood that students and parents feared the results. For that we have some misinformed educators to blame.

Even today there is a huge bureaucracy that sets academic standards. In a recent instance, the New York State Education Department refused to change the grading scale on a regents exam failed by an inordinate amount of students, including those considered to be in the top levels. After countless complaints from many school districts, all of which favored a change and an outburst from parents and students whose lives could be changed by their actions, the bureaucrats still refused to yield. "It's not possible to change an exam score as long as it has gone through the proper pretesting!" Another job well done by our bureaucrats. Keep these people in mind. They are the ones who judge your children. I don't want to seem prejudiced. So I thought you would find it amusing that a state teachers' certification exam taken by 1800 licensed and practicing teachers had a 50% failure rate. Here, however, the powers at the state level were pressured to lower the grading curve and they acquiesced.

There is a major difference in this case as opposed to the student test mentioned above. Here, in New York State, there are unions, and unions mean votes, and votes are lures (bait) for politicians to encircle like a pack of animals hovering over a recently killed carcass. The point is that the very teachers who are judging our children according to state standards are themselves being evaluated at below acceptable grade levels. In the case I cited, teacher complaints were accommodated. The teacher union had more political clout than the students whom they taught. There are many different forms of intelligence, but unfortunately, we only talk about one.

Many people who have not scored well on these IQ exams have reached goals in every field of life, outstripping the scores that allegedly doomed them. As I have noted, low IQ scores have no direct correlation with the ability to learn or achieve and many have far surpassed those with high scores. I am living proof of that. Intelligence comes in many forms. Those who score high on these IQ tests certainly do possess

LABELING

a gift. You will find no low IQs among scientists, doctors, Supreme Court justices, and although in many cases it is well camouflaged, United States presidents. We can all reflect on situations where decisions by judges have been appalling and lacked a connection to reality, same for doctors and presidents. They may have high IQs, but they lack smarts in the realm of the real world. For example, a federal judge ruled in favor of a pedophile, allowing him to keep sexually explicit pornography displayed on his cell walls. He challenged the state to produce definitive studies showing a therapeutic basis for the restriction of this pornography although there were outcries and political interference. The judge stood his ground. This is only one example out of thousands made by judges who have tenured positions for life. Power without accountability leads to destructive decisions. This is a clear case of someone who possesses a high IQ but has no ability to think creatively. Make no mistake about it, there are truck drivers, mail carriers, laborers, homeless and ghetto dwellers that have extremely high IQs but have never used their talents, for whatever reason, to better their lives.

Not all people with high IQs achieve, and conversely, there are probably more people with low IQ scores that do achieve. One must possess certain qualities to build successful businesses, perform for an audience, or create a piece of art. These qualities require an intellect much different than those tested by our educators for their IQ. A native shrewdness, an insight, a vivid imagination, a keen sense of timing: people who possess these and many other qualities when compared to their high IQ peers far surpass them in the world of business. However, when you mix the two, you get a perfect balance. Make no mistake about it, having a high IQ without the other qualities gives birth to such a term as *"nerd."*

There are no IQ exams to test these people and the countless other qualities of genius that a myriad of people posses. An IQ cannot measure qualities that Michael Jordan, Derrick Jeter, master craftsmen, and a host of others posses. These are people who have talents that reside in parts of the human brain that are not evaluated by an IQ test. Do not let anyone tell you that the genius you enjoy is not equal to or better than the genius our intellectuals have. It is just a different type of genius.

Standardized testing is questionable at best. The New York State English Regents provides a perfect example. McGraw-Hill for New York has developed the test for the state. It is a six-hour examination that requires four essays. Scoring of the test is by a rubric and scoring matrix provided by the state. If a student had a 75 on the examination in the previous year, in the current year, because of changes in the matrix, it would be an 85. In fact, the matrix can and does change each year. This way the state controls not only the grading process but also the number of students passing and the number achieving mastery. Why? Obviously, if the test is needed for graduation and large numbers are failing, the scoring can be adjusted to ensure how many pass and how many fail. If one wanted to be cynical about it the fact that the city schools do much more poorly than the suburban schools on the exam, means the state has to compensate for the failure rate in the cities of New York by fudging the exam grades. Hence, huge numbers of unqualified seniors graduate when they have not met minimal standards. The

LABELING

examinations they take become the principal factor in the lives of marginal students. Nothing they have done in the past counts only the grade on the required Regents exam. Suffice to say, the pressure is enormous. True learning often gives way to cramming and memorizing. Without acceptable scores on these exams, students cannot advance their educations.

The people who design, grade, and administer these exams operate in a world outside the classroom and outside of any criticism. They have complete autonomy. Certainly, it is our youth the schools must focus on. Have a child who is having problems coping, constantly rebelling, and showing his displeasure with school? Wake up and read the signs. He is frustrated with himself and the system. He feels helpless. The Department of Education and individual teachers try to deal with these problems, but they do not have all the answers.

You must help! First you must understand the problem yourself. It takes compassion, patience, understanding, and much quality time. Most of all it takes "change"; change in your approach and attitude. Do not expect the child to approach you. You must approach him. The results are worth all the efforts. Not only will your children be rewarded and lead a more fruitful and less frustrating life but the country will reap the rewards of this added brain trust coming online with all its contributions. Again, all we are doing is reprogramming the brain with positive thoughts until the negativity and the stigma is removed. The power of positive thinking will always prove successful. Finally, we need an approach that will reach people in the ghettos and many others who are less fortunate and are unable to seek the proper help. It will unleash a vast amount of brainpower into society heretofore wasted; it all begins at home.

Notes

Misguided Use of Brainpower
The Need for Reprogramming Brains

As we make our way through life, one of the more frustrating things we have to deal with is politics and the political system. Virtually everything falls prey to our political structure and how it is managed. Let me make it crystal clear that I am proud to be an American, but we have serious problems that need serious attention.

The system that our government administers is rooted in the democratic ideal. No other country in the world has as many checks and balances or as many political representatives from diverse backgrounds. Our political structure is designed to ensure that our country is managed by the people, for the people, and of the people, regardless of race, color, or creed. Unfortunately, the manner in which our politicians administer our country is far from what was anticipated by the Founding Fathers. Now, government is more often for the politicians, by the politicians, and of the politicians.

The problem with our leaders is that they are so busy working on reelection they will say what people want to hear while making private deals to benefit themselves. We shiver at the thought of dictatorship, yet our government has created many autonomous agencies and each and every one of them is its own dictatorship with almost unlimited powers.

We are mere pawns struggling to exist in a society so corrupt that corruption is a way of life accepted by most of us. We all remember Frank Serpico. Singlehandedly, he exposed the fraud being perpetrated by the police force from the highest-ranking officer's right down through the ranks. After much hullabaloo, the one who suffered the most was Serpico himself. He had to go into hiding in fear of his own life.

From the IRS, FBI, HUD, FDA, FAA, Welfare, army, navy, senate, congress, cabinet, the White House staff, and the president himself, corruption was rampant. What is worse is that the perpetrators are always protected by the power bestowed upon them through these autonomous agencies. The only ones who suffer are the pawns, and in many cases, these pawns, you and I, are singled out to take the rap. Frequently, we are judged guilty by the press, another autonomous power-wielding group, and then handed over to some power-hungry DA who cares more about winning the case for his own advancement than the truth. Recently, public hearings highlighted a litany of taxpayer abuses suffered at the hands of overly aggressive IRS agents. Stories have been told of people having their lives literally ruined by wrongful conduct of these agents. Yet not one agent has been held accountable for his actions. Not one taxpayer has had reparations for his damages or even received apologies.

Purportedly, these congressional hearings were to produce a more just and friendly atmosphere for the taxpayer. However, it seems they were more like window dressing by our politicians. What was the actual goal then? I leave that for you to conclude. The FBI crime lab has been found guilty of tampering with evidence. This tampering has made certain cases impossible to adjudicate fairly. The inescapable conclusion is that they sacrificed integrity and objectivity in pursuit of convictions and then tried to cover up. None of the FBI agents involved in these horrific acts was properly punished even though they were responsible for crimes that you or I would go to jail for. How many politicians do you know in the history of our country that have committed crimes and gone to trial as compared to how many should have gone to trial? More discouraging is their punishment: usually reelection. Ted Kennedy, Marion Barry, and countless others are perfect examples of wrong behavior being rewarded.

Countless deaths have occurred because industrial leaders, who financially support our politicians, have allowed faulty products to remain on the market because of its cost benefit. Once discovered, the company is fined the money goes to some government agency, and the next day it is business as usual; no one is tried for murder.

Time after time we have heard of cars being recalled for faulty equipment. Some of these recalls have been very serious problems, i.e., faulty gas tanks that have blown up on impact and have killed people. It is common knowledge that General Motors knew of such a problem but when the bean counters (accountants) figured the cost of recall against the cost of settling lawsuits, the decision was to keep quiet and ignore the problem even though people might have been killed. No one went to jail.

Why do we, the people of the strongest and freest country in the world, accept this behavior? Because our brains have been programmed to shrug it off: "That's politics." "That's politics" is a very scary thought especially in such a volatile environment. If our politicians don't change and stop acting for the benefit of their own partisan views, if our many agencies heretofore mentioned don't change their tactics and begin interplaying not only with the public but themselves, if these changes do not occur, our country will awaken to disastrous times. We cannot continue to exist as we are.

People, we must wake up! We must program the brains of our youth whether they are black, white, rich, or poor. We must use every resource we have from the ghetto to society hill. We must teach our youth how to be leaders of the future and through this leadership improve the lifestyles of all our people. After all, if there were oil under the ground in Harlem, we would pour millions of dollars into extracting this resource from the ground, even though it is in a blighted area. Why not spend the same money extracting their brainpower, which could benefit society much more than the oil?

As I noted previously, nothing happens without an image or a dream and to quote Martin Luther King Jr., "I have a dream." But that is not enough. We all need to have a dream, and once that dream becomes affixed in our minds, it can then become a reality. Wake up, America; we must become the agent of reprogramming.

Notes

The Disease of Rehabilitation or the Lack Thereof

While speaking about reprogramming brains, a question comes to mind. Isn't that what prisons are supposed to do? The mere existence of today's prisons is a threat to society. The criminal element, which is allowed to flourish behind these walls, has little in the way of rehabilitation. On the contrary, prisons release inmates more hostile than when they entered, and certainly with many more contacts in the underground world than before. How can a parole board, another autonomous group, release killers, rapists, and muggers just because they spent time behind bars? They have not been programmed to fit into society. They have not been placed into environments that are destined to cultivate a new attitude, yet they are let loose and many end up harming innocent people. We have to rethink these institutions and make prisons a place to rehabilitate those willing to embrace change and forever incarcerate the sociopathic recidivists.

Judges and parole boards are in important positions. They owe society the protection it deserves. They are a direct link to the criminals and the prisons. Judges and parole boards release countless prisoners with records of repeated abuses.

THE DISEASE OF REHABILITATION OR THE LACK THEREOF

When returned to society, many of these prisoners continue their criminal acts some even taking the lives of others. Rarely has a judge or parole board been held accountable.

Has anyone emerged to create or to lead a battle for total prison reform? Not to my knowledge and if so, such reform has not been successful. Where are the people we need for this work? What are they doing to help society address this issue? Are the managers of the prison system and the judiciary meeting their responsibilities? And if they are not, let's hold them accountable for their inaction. After all, it's your life and my life at stake here. We do not need another brain trust of intelligent people with high IQs who are complacent in their positions and unwilling to press their imaginations to the limits for the betterment of society.

Notes

Change: The Key to Self-Satisfaction

Change is a word that rolls off our tongues without the slightest notion of how to implement it. For a word so commonly used and so easily defined, it represents one of the most difficult things man is called upon to do, "*change.*"

In order to accomplish change, we must know what it is we want to change. In addition, most important, what is the result we are looking to accomplish? Every attempt to change must have a goal. This is the key to success. No goal, no success. This idea returns us to one of my previous remarks. Before we attempt to start any type of change, we must contemplate our goal. After all, one does not start a journey without first knowing his destination. When Tiger Woods was once asked, "What do you think of before you hit the ball?"

"Where it will land?" replied the superstar, confirming my theory of knowing your destination and then planting the image in your mind.

Imagery, imagination, there are those words again, the use of our brain to reprogram itself. Everyone reading this treatise has tried change. Whether it is changing bad habits, such as smoking, eating, or something more profound, you are playing with the same brain and the same principle.

Eating and smoking are good examples. A vast number of people have attempted to change one or both of these habits, but the failure rate in terms of change is extremely high and understandably so. To stop smoking or overeating, like anything else requires a singular mind-set. It takes change. There is no easy way, and any shortcuts offered are in most cases commercially driven and result in failure.

Imagine yourself in the hospital, tubes in and out of your body, attached to life support apparatus, fighting lung cancer, and then succumbing to an early death, denying you and your family the pleasures of life. On the other hand, imagine yourself smoke-free, in good health, vacationing with the family, making that 8:30 tee-off time, and living a healthy, fruitful life with much to look forward to. Once these images are indelibly affixed in your mind, the smoking will stop and the stronger the positive image the better the chances for success. No goal, no image, no success. To stop smoking, like anything else, we must change. Program the mind and never stop imagining success.

The majority of people trying to lose weight have no understanding of what they are doing, resulting in a failure rate second to none. Losing weight is much different than losing fat and building muscle mass. Most people go on some kind of commercial supplement or diet with the goal of shedding "X" amount of pounds. Therefore, like puppets, they follow this plan, struggling to reach the desired weight, and if by chance they reach the targeted weight loss, they have already failed. In addition, they are doing harm to their bodies. What they want to do is lose fat and add muscle mass. This could add weight since muscle is heavier than fat, but the body will be toned and look thinner. Proper eating habits, not diets, along with an exercise program will result in the loss of unwanted fat and inches off the waist and hips and give an individual the body he wants.

When dieting through the use of pills or some temporary, short-term eating plan, we do lose weight, and most of the weight we lose is muscle mass. It is protein, not fat.

People who lose weight in this fashion are usually in and out of these fads the rest of their lives. Those who may achieve the desired weight loss are disappointed when viewing the results. No muscle mass, no tone, loose, flopping skin not exactly what the advertisement looked like. What's worse is that when weight is put back on, which is inevitable as soon as an individual goes off the program, the weight returns as fat and never replaces the muscle mass or protein that was lost during the diet.

Sorry, folks. No tricks, no shortcuts. Scanning over-the-counter drugs and diet plans should convince anyone that this multimillion-dollar business just does not work. Losing weight, like smoking, or any other desired achievement, is a mind-set, a change in one's lifestyle and eating habits. One must look in a mirror every day, imagine what he wants his body to look like, and with that picture sculpted into the mind begin a long-term journey, slowly changing his eating habits while adopting a lifestyle that includes an exercise program. Short of this, my advice is to stay fat. The process of losing and gaining weight is bad for your heart and reduces muscle mass.

Notes

Helping Others Requires Changes Within

What is more difficult is when we are called upon to help others, usually loved ones, suffering, in situations where suffering is not necessary. There are situations where people suffer deep psychological problems because the brain is deficient in its operation. I am not a doctor of any kind, and I do not make the claim that my methods will cure any of these situations, which often can be best handled by professionals. However, if the professional included some kind of positive imagery, I am sure it would help speed the recovery.

We, as parents, who have children suffering from poor self-images, from being learning disabled, or from having physical inadequacies are responsible for guiding our children on a realistic path of achievement, we have a moral responsibility to help. However, before helping our children, we must help ourselves. Are we talking about some kind of "change" here? We sure are, and it is as difficult as I mentioned previously. We must change our approach, change our attitude, and change our method of communication before we attempt to help anyone.

Children in need of help will let you know so by their actions. Cantankerousness, moodiness, shyness, and belligerence are some of the signs children give to their parents. How else can a parent expect troubled children to ask for help? You are the role model; you have to reach them. They cannot and do not know how else to reach you except in behaviors that attract attention.

Our natural instinct is to react to our children in the same fashion they display. We lash back with anger at their actions, saying hurtful things that further exacerbate the situation and, worse than that, feed more negativity to a child who is already overwhelmed with enough pain. This kind or reaction drives a wedge a little deeper each time between you and your child. You are not acting as a parent; you are a truant officer. In most cases, love between a child and a parent is a given, but trust and respect are earned. Until your child trusts and respects you, all your efforts are for naught. Remember you can love someone without always respecting his opinion.

When a child displays an unacceptable attitude, a smart parent seizes the situation as an opportunity to help, an opportunity to feed positive thoughts of love and devotion to the child. To continually build one child's confidence with superlatives while discussing negative actions in a loving and humble way, such parents will help get to the root of the problem, which in most cases will be some form of poor self-image or a more profound mental disorder.

One thing also must be emphasized; I know you hear what your child is saying, but are you listening? Remember, if your attitude and method of handling your child does not change, neither will they. As a parent, find the cause; don't attack the problem. It only makes things worse.

Many of us do not understand the difference between hearing and listening. This is the most common reason for

HELPING OTHERS REQUIRES CHANGES WITHIN

most relationships going astray. We tend to hear what our children or spouses say, but too often we don't take the time to listen and understand their point of view.

If we can't learn to step back and understand what they are trying to communicate, the consequences, sooner or later, are usually devastating.

Inadequate athletic or physical limitations, difficulty in school, social dysfunction are the things that most commonly affect our children. Through the process of active listening, a poor self-image can be changed, and unbelievable breakthroughs will occur.

Sometimes we accomplish everything just by working on one thing. For example, a child who has negative thoughts about his athleticism or physical demeanor can carry a negative, uncomplimentary feeling of himself into every walk of life. Through your understanding of the situation, martial arts or weight lifting can be an answer. Martial arts and bodybuilding are sports as well as body- and mind-enhancing activities. Someone accomplished in martial arts or bodybuilding will certainly have a positive feeling about how these disciplines can promote self-image and replace any negativity. There are many other activities that will do the job. You will be guided by your understanding, your ability to relate your success in earning the child's trust and respect. Only with this team effort, along with all the other methods of imagery previously discussed, will success be found.

If school happens to be a major problem, then support everything else the child does. Show him how he shines in other areas and outperforms students with better grades. Get extra help and make learning fun. Do not make the child feel that anything less than an A or B is unacceptable. Grades are meaningless and have very little to do with reality. The grading system is a subjective process administered by instructors with varying requirements; remember the Einsteins of the world. Einstein, you will recall, was almost mute until he was five and was a serious cause of concern to his parents and, later in his life, to his teachers. His unique genius was not recognized until he was in his twenties. Anyone can learn. It just depends on the teacher. Teaching is not a science. It is an art. It is an individual interaction between two people. That interaction is different for everyone. A good teacher will find a way to relate. You, as the parent, hold the responsibility of being that teacher.

One of the best ways to improve one's learning ability is to improve his reading skills. There are many methods offered. Just choose one that best fits your child's needs.

So if you do nothing else, teach your child to read. Make it a fun thing. They are never too young or too old for reading. Today's theory is to read to our children from birth. Some even believe learning starts while the child is still in the womb. This is another sign of how powerful the brain truly is.

Remember, doing poorly in school generates negative feelings about oneself. We must overcome the negativity before we see achievement. "Change" the mind from a fear of losing to no fear of winning, something we are all capable of doing once our mind is set and the image is clear.

43. *"A good reader is a good learner. There are experts that say, 'Give me a good reader and the rest is easy.'"*

Notes

Conclusion

It is interesting to note that at this point in my writings, Derrick Jeter has announced his retirement, and he has become the greatest baseball player who has won the hearts of many people around the world. Suffice it to say, his popularity is well deserved, and of course, his parents are the cause; he is the effect. As I listen and read various experts comment on his success, I notice each and every one of them marvels at his personal demeanor and lifestyle as well as his athletic ability. As I have already stated, focus is an ally too powerful for any opponent. However, the point to be made here is that Derek Jeter is the result of loving and devoted parents who trained his mind to focus and remain positive. Through their devotion, proper guidance, and love, they slowly but surely gained his respect. If by now you have not understood why he is so widely loved, it is because, besides being one of the most accomplished players in history, he has a demeanor that commands respect. What a combination: superior talent and extreme humility. A profile of a person that only exists through the power of positive thinking and positive and powerful parental support.

Some parents feel that a child's anger, fear, or sadness is a threat, a challenge to authority evidence of the parents' incompetence. Others see these negative emotions as a

CONCLUSION

cry for help and a perfect chance to become closer and an opportunity to guide them into making progress and positive decisions. Children of parents who have positive attitudes about developing their child's emotional life are more successful both in and out of school. As a parent, you are an "emotional coach."

One must focus on life. Too often we wear blinders and suffer from tunnel vision. Success cannot be measured by the mere gathering of wealth, which by itself can be an empty achievement. To be successful, one must be self-satisfied. To achieve that, all the other elements of life have to be successful: family, relationships, health, appearance, and social and economic performance. It's your total contribution to humanity that measures a person's success. That contribution begins with feeling good about ones self. Accomplishing a totally successful life starts with an image of what you want to be and then "just doing it."

What I am attempting to accomplish through this writing is to share with you the concept of brainpower, a power without equal. I have discussed many topics; all centered about brain programming. The central concept I have advocated is that through my techniques and unrelenting determination, anything that is programmed can be reprogrammed. To accomplish any goal requires change. If you change your thinking patterns, while following my philosophy, you have a fine chance to succeed at life. Remember, *44. "Failure and success are states of mind; therefore, you are neither until you decide you are."* How many times will a baby trip and fall before it walks? Expect to trip, fall, and regress. It's not how many times you fall that counts, it's how many times you get up.

Notes

A Personal Vision

As I enter the twenty-first century in the sixth decade of my life, I consider both my past and the future. I see the past as the bedrock for those things I still wish to achieve, for I have been chiseled out of this stone into the person I am today. Whatever my virtues are, whatever my strengths are, whatever my human frailties are have come from this sculpting. Now, with the payload of the past and with this book, I embark on a new voyage, a new journey. For I have come to understand that what is meaningful in life is what is shared. Whether it is love, joy, or sorrow, what is shared gives life one of its most fundamental values. And so, for me, sharing the lessons I have learned from both defeat and success, from wrestling with eccentricities of life, is the best course I can take in my life. Now I would like to give to each of you, my readers and friends, and to all of those whom I have yet to encounter, the hard won lessons of my life. I would like to give you the wellspring of my strength when faced with adversity. I would like to give you my insights into our world and illustrate how to not only survive in it, but prosper. I have the deepest faith that within us is the power to change our lives both physically and mentally. I believe that is true for you, and I believe that it is true for me.

In order for me to go forth on this adventure, I must leave the world that has nourished me for most of my adult life and enter a new world, a world of unknowns. It is there where I shall bring my message of the triumph of the human spirit. I shall bring that word to all of those who are willing to listen. Let that be my legacy more than the land I have developed or the dollars I have earned. Let my energy and love of life flow outward and embrace all of you who would drink this nectar. For each of you, the future you want lies within your grasp. Let me show you the path.

Notes

As you were reading this book, I created some quotes, and like any form of art, they are always open to interpretation. I would like to share with you my insights, my perceptions, my visions, and my interpretations of each quote, and I invite you to do the same.

Quotes from the Book

1) "The similarity between success and failure is one's state of mind."
2) "The worst day of your life is a welcome substitute for your last days."
3) "To achieve in life, one must know his goal."
4) "Appreciate what you have rather than agonize over what you do not have."
5) "There are many people who are *wealthier* than me, but few are *richer*."
6) "It is not how often you fall that counts; it is how often you rise."
7) "You are what you believe. You can be what you imagine."

QUOTES

8) "It is not circumstances that shapes our minds, but our reaction to it."
9) "Success has a unique meaning for each of us."
10) "Nothing is real and everything is perception."
11) "Not all who can see have vision."
12) "Youth is wasted on youth unless we chose to embrace it."
13) "When emotions control actions, the results are brainless."
14) "Weakness is a poison, which is a failure of the mind."
15) "I wish I was to the sphere, as I am to the circle."
16) "Unbridled passion can make us vulnerable."
17) "In life we shed our past and go through rebirth. The only constant is our soul."
18) "Listen to a man's words, but give his actions more value before you give him respect."
19) "Dreams are as real as we make them, and the more we believe in them, the more attainable they become."
20) "Gather all the wisdom of the universe as we travel through space and time and make it a part of our journey here on this planet."
21) "Hurt can only occur if there is intent; otherwise it is a misperception."
22) "Man is a computer. His brain is the processor. Alter the processor and you change the man."
23) "The heartless man said, 'You will lose much sleep if you loan money to friends and unknowns.' The caring man said, 'I will lose more if I do not.'"

24) "It is unfortunate that the wisdom of the aged cannot be transferred to the recklessness of youth."
25) "Evil rots the core of society."
26) 'The eye cannot see what the heart feels."
27) "Another man's success is only an image that reality can shatter."
28) "The ability to achieve is as limitless as your ability to imagine."
29) "When the heart is empty, we are alone."
30) "To live only in the world and not the imagination is to waste God's gift to us."
31) "Stupidity is most dangerous when we will not admit to it."
32) "Friendship is based on a perception of what is. Only in time of need is the true measure of friendship known."
33) "Love scorned is attacked by ego and emotion, and emotions have no brain."
34) "If God created what man can overcome, can God be among the living?"
35) "Listening to the problems of others trivializes our own, but really helps to change or comfort us."
36) "One's desires cannot come before one's needs."
37) "Love comes in many packages. It's the wrapping that attracts but the content that is meaningful."
38) "Program your processor with positive power and see the results."
39) "To love is to enjoy the pleasures of one another."
40) "Believe in what you see, but what you see is an image of what you believe."

QUOTES

41) "We are all born with love; we learn about evil."
42) "Praying is a form of imagery since what we are praying for is not yet attained."
43) "A good reader is a good learner. There are experts that say, 'Give me a good reader and the rest is easy.'"
44) "Failure and success are states of mind; therefore, you are neither until you decide you are."
45) "Life is like a boomerang; whatever you throw out there will always return."

1) *"The similarity between success and failure is one's state of mind."*

There is a phrase that I like to use, "Show me a successful person and I will show you a failure."

What that means is that a majority of people who have attained success have experienced failure.

If one was to look the word *failure* up in the dictionary, two definitions would appear: the first being very simplistic, i.e., heart failure, kidney failure, etc. The second is as quoted, "Defeat, collapse, the condition or fact of not achieving the desired end!"

However, my definition looks at failure in a totally different way. Failure is the gateway to success.

By analyzing the facts, which led to your present situation, one learns important lessons on what to or not do going forward.

If we use this knowledge, pick ourselves up, and march forward, then we didn't fail; we hit a detour and gained knowledge on how to avoid what did not work, and like any detour in the road, we proceed with our journey just in a different way but always with the same goal in mind.

So remember, failure could be considered the other side of success.

2) *"The worst day of your life is a welcome substitute for your last days."*

Whoever said life would be easy? Like the saying goes, we don't get a book of instructions at birth.

Upon waking up in the morning, all of us begin to agonize over the many different problems we need to face, along with the ones that have not yet reared there head, but we know they will.

Many of us will allow these problems to captivate our minds, occupy our time, and fantasize about the harsh results (which are usually always wrong). We treat these problems so seriously that they actually become who we are and cause damaging effects on our personalities, our health, and everyone near and dear to us. In short, we become our problems.

Whatever your problems are today if solved will be replaced by others tomorrow and if not solved will be added to the new ones we acquire almost on a daily basis.

We must stop using the word *problems*. We don't have "problems," we have a series of life situations.

Yes, the water gets rough, the sea will swell, and the ship will rock. You might suffer a slight temporary reaction, but we know the calm is just ahead.

No matter what your goal is in life, you will always face life's situations. Our goal in life is to handle and solve to the best of our ability that which confronts us, not allowing us to drown in rough seas.

Don't allow your problems (situations) to control your life and define who you are.

I guarantee that someday when age or sickness sets in and the end looks closer than further away, you would substitute your worst day of your problems for the present situation.

Live a happy and successful life, handle your everyday situations with strength and positivity—this will allow all of your other phases of life, family, friends, etc., to be more enjoyable. "Don't die before you're dead."

3) *"To achieve in life, one must know his goal."*

He kicks off on the twenty-yard line. The ball is kicked as far and as high as possible to allow his teammates time to charge down the field looking like a herd of giants merging in and focusing on obliterating the receiver.

The receiver would be obliterated if it weren't for his teammates of giants running down the field so they can meet head-on almost literally, like two Roman armies in the old days. At the same time, the receiver is amongst the mayhem dodging in and out around or over if necessary—he has but one thought on his mind and only one thing—to get that ball over that goal line.

Hit him, push him, kick him, tackle him, flat on his face—but the one thing we know is he will get up, shake it off, and do it again and again as many times as needed until he reaches that goal line. We can all picture what I am saying; we see it every week. They get banged around more times than not by many more. Then one of the giants limp off the field, and several plays later returns to the battlegrounds to do it all over again.

This is an example of what having a goal in life is all about.

Without setting goals, we lose our determination and our focus.

The receiver on the football team has one goal, and that goal is so fixed in his mind that failure is not an option, no matter what it takes or the roadblocks along the way. Nothing is stopping him.

Determine your goals in every phase of life, health, as well as family and career, focus and expect a tough journey, and never give up. I promise with that determination you will achieve your goals, for failure's not an option.

4) *"Appreciate what you have rather than agonize over what we do not have."*

If man were born with sonar, rather than eyes, we might be a lot more harmonious with each other.

What I am trying to say is by seeing and observing your surroundings, we have a tendency of comparing our possessions with others.

However, what you see is not reality; it is only your perception.

Over the years, I have come to realize that all the people I envied eventually disappointed me.

You must begin to take stock of yourself. We must realize that things have no emotions and can never satisfy one's life.

Most of us are so busy complaining about what we don't have that we cannot appreciate what we do have, the things others cannot see.

In evaluating our lives, the things we have are those that are visual and those that are not apparent.

Visual assessment is comparing our home, furniture, cars, and all other tangible material objects. Just keep in mind there are countless amount of people in this world that would in turn envy your position in life.

What no one can compare is our true blessings—health, family, relationships, etc.

Agonizing over if you do or do not have negates the pleasure of enjoying what you and your family have given up to build what you do have.

Envy is a cancer, and it not only spreads through our minds and bodies, but it's contagious by those closest, like family.

Improving our life is not without changes. Change the way you look at things and the things you look at will change and at that point you will begin to enjoy what you worked so hard to have.

Stop agonizing over what you do or don't have instead enjoy what you are blessed with.

This is how to achieve inner strength and peace of mind.

5) *"There are many people who are wealthier than me, but few are richer."*

According to the dictionary, *wealth* and *rich* are synonyms. I, however, have my own definition for rich.

We judge people's success by the wealth they are perceived to have. Again, wealth and success are perceived by most as synonymous.

What is wealth? While talking to a group of college students, one asked, "How do you get wealthy like you?"

I answered, "How much is wealthy to you?"

He replied with, "You know, a lot of money."

So again, I asked, "What is a lot of money?"

You see that answer to that question differs with each individual. Michael Jackson made hundreds of millions, and he went broke from overspending. On the other hand, we all know people who live on so much less yet they pay their bills on time and sustain a normal life. So then I ask you, "Who is wealthier?"

So as far as wealthier goes, never compare yourself to anyone; there will always be someone with more and others with less.

My definition for *rich* is synonymous with *wealth* but only in the category of money and other tangible objects.

Rich is having many other things needed for quality of life. Rich is having besides just money a healthy lifestyle; a tight, close family with much love; and an ability to be humble to others. Being rich is not only being loved but being respected. Thus, strive at being the richest person not the wealthiest.

6) *As quoted by many, "It is not how often you fall that counts; it is how often you rise."*

There is nothing in life that will guarantee your success other than not being able to rise above your failures and learn from your past mistakes. As long as you are in forward motion, there is no way you can fail. Success is all in your hands. It is all in your mind-set. It is all in your desire, your work ethic, and most importantly, your ability to rise above and start over as many times as needed to achieve desired success.

7) *"You are what you believe. You can be what you imagine."*

Think of the word *believe*. We all have beliefs. Listening to every pontificating on their beliefs each contradicting the next leads one to wonder who is right and who is wrong.

Total confusion is different beliefs being bandied around. How do people make decisions or choices? It is these clashes and beliefs that keep our government from working together in harmony.

If we step back for a moment and realize that a belief is nothing more than one's opinion, this would bring us to the conclusion that there is no right or wrong. The rhetoric we are subjected to by our politics for example—gay marriage, abortion, sixteen-ounce soda consumption, etc.—are all born from party believers clashing with each other.

So I think we can conclude that one's belief is only a reality to one's self. We have so many beliefs ingrained into us by who we associate with and when packaged together those beliefs define who we are.

Keep in mind that beliefs are not reality to anyone but yourself. Every belief we have is a function of our imagination. The power of our beliefs differs. Some we are willing to debate and others are so affixed in our mind that discussions are not an option.

If you now agree that our beliefs are nothing more than a figment of our imagination, you are steps closer to having the ability to change your life and team goals here too for not attainable.

Most of us are like a tire spinning in the snow. No matter how much gas we give it, the tires keep spinning and the car stays in a rut.

Eventually we realize we are getting nowhere and believe what we are doing is waning. This belief leads us to change our strategy. We use a different approach and finally through changing our belief, which leads us to take a different approach, we break through and once again we are back on the road to our destination.

We all have the power to change our beliefs and use our imagination to obtain a new you.

Imagine yourself, think of what your goals in life are, imagine what you want to be, who you want to be, how you want to look, make a total picture of your new image and believe that it is who you are not who you are going to be, but imagine you are that person today. Never, never falter on your belief that this new image is who you are today.

You will be surprised to realize "you are what you believe and the result is determined by your imagination."

8) *"It is not circumstances that shapes our minds, but our reaction to it."*

You're sitting, minding your own business, and suddenly you're approached by an annoying intruder. Faced with a circumstance appearing instantaneously, we must react.

Reaction to a circumstance in some cases are physical, others are emotional. Some are instantaneous and others justify deeper thought as to our reaction.

One thing is for sure. We all face many different circumstances and actions to them on an everyday basis.

There are no sets of rules on how to react to these circumstances. However your reaction could change the rest of your life, in some cases for the good and some for the worse.

Our reaction is based on our emotions in many cases and not our brains. Emotions have no brains and in most cases lead us to negative results.

Circumstances that don't require immediate action give us a chance to think and prepare for our reaction, which in all cases is a safer situation than emotional outbreak.

Countless amounts of people have experienced life-changing events by just one emotional outbreak that could have easily been avoided using brains instead of emotions.

A negative reaction to a circumstance is a brainless decision made by our ego, another brainless reaction is when our ego is attached. It is only you who can determine the action, so it is not the circumstances that shape us it is our actions to it.

9) *"Success has a unique meaning for each of us."*

Success is a very personal set of achievements. We generally attribute success to the wealth of an individual.

Shallow as that maybe it is the common belief; however, many of us realize that having an empire of wealth is absolutely not synonymous with success.

There are many people who can buy and sell you, afford the most expensive cars, houses, and all the other frills that life can offer.

This is a wonderful achievement, but if its comes with a bag full of family problems, worn health, and a bunch of other unwelcome situations, we might want to rethink our definition of success.

When one gets the opportunity to really look into some of the lives of people they think are considered a success, their opinions of the meaning of success will change.

Success is an individual evaluation of who we are, what we have, its how we feel about our entire life. Therefore, success has a unique meaning for each of us.

10) *"Nothing is real and everything is perception."*

Go to a movie, see a show, or read a book. Discuss any of the above with others sharing the same experience and you might feel they are not referring to the same thing you saw.

Reality is a statement of how we see or interpret things and how we interpret things is a result of how we perceive what we see.

We all view what we see different from one another. People have their own perception of what they are viewing.

This difference is what makes some art worth more than others, some people better looking than others, etc. The true fact is nothing is real; everything is perception.

11) *"Not all who can see have vision."*

Those of us born with eyes use those eyes to view the world.

Sight is a gift. It allows us to appreciate a multitude of gifts the world has to offer. Sight is not something we have to learn. It is part of our everyday function and in many cases taken for granted.

Sight, however, is not the same as vision. Yes, in many circumstances one might refer to "how is your vision," they are referring to your sight; but vision takes on a deeper meaning.

Vision is the ability to gather all of what you have seen, all that you have experienced, and all the knowledge you have accumulated.

Through the years, we gather and store information into our subconscious mind. It is this subconscious mind that gives us vision or the ability not only to see what we see but to draw conclusions by drawing from our past experience. This is what gives us the vision.

Vision is the ability to create a picture of future results as to what the eye has seen. Not all who can see has vision.

"Youth is wasted on youth unless they choose to embrace it."

QUOTES

12) *"Youth is wasted on youth unless we chose to embrace it."*

Youth is a journey into the future. We are all in a rush to reach our destination, but it's not the destination that counts, it is the journey that counts. And if we don't enjoy the journey, then we have wasted our youth.

13) *"When emotions control actions, the results are brainless."*

Actions and reactions are part of our everyday life. All of us experienced unpleasant situation, some more than others.
Life is one without restraint, control, and reaction.
It is the reaction that we must focus on. When our ego is attacked, in many cases we allow our emotions to control our actions.
We see how families that split up and their damaged ego turns their house into a battleground with no consideration for the suffering children it's only about them.
People fight, kill, die, and go to jail because they lost control of their emotions.
We are all responsible for our actions, and we have a responsibility to ourselves and others to control emotions because they have no brains.

14) *"Weakness is a poison, which is a failure of the mind."*

Everything we do emanates from the brain. The brain is weak. If it gives into adversity, the body is poisoned and reacts accordingly. The only antidote is reprogramming your mind to positive thoughts.

15) *"I wish I was to the sphere, as I am to the circle."*

People by nature are always looking at what they don't have. This is not always a bad thing if they processed correctly what you see.

Whether we realize it or not, our main goal in life is to achieve an inner feeling of contentment.

Contentment is an individual fulfillment and only you know when that goal has been accomplished.

We achieve this inner peace by constantly comparing our present position with that of others. If what we see creates envy, then we rot and never rise above the circle we have created. However, if what we see encourages us to work harder and consistently strive for a new goal, climb from our circle to another level, then we had reached the sphere and now you are to the sphere what you were to your circle.

16) *"Unbridled passion can make us vulnerable."*

There is no greater experience in life than that of passion. Passion can drive us to heights we never considered possible. Passion can also open one up for disaster and much heartache.

When we think of passion, we relate it to either a feeling for another or an inner drive to achieve at a chosen activity, i.e., music, sports, etc.

Whichever we are experiencing, passion is a deep emotional feeling. In order to succeed, we must open up to the world how and what we are feeling. Since we agree that passion is our deepest emotional feeling, rejection in many cases can destroy us, thus unbridled passion can make us vulnerable.

17) *"In life we shed our past and go through rebirth. The only constant is our soul."*

Look back at the early years of your life. Think of all the different stages you have been through from birth, to crawling, to walking, preschool, kindergarten, grade school, high school, college, marriage, having children, the world of business, and now heading toward the golden years. All these can be considered stages of your life. Each of these stages was a prerequisite to the other. As we pass from one stage to the other, in effect we are having a rebirth by shedding the past and entering into a new future. Through life we process our experiences, gather knowledge and wisdom, and move ahead the one thing that is a constant is the soul. If we do objectionable things from phase to phase, we might be able to still advance in the growth of life, but we can't change our soul. Our deeds will always be reflected in our soul, so although we shed our past and go through the rebirth, the only constant is our soul.

18) *"Listen to man's words, but give his actions more value before you give him respect."*

Time after time, we listen to people, both friends and strangers, so much is said and we hear their words, but we have no idea if their actions are parallel to what they say.

Suffice it to say, the easiest example is backed up all the promises spread from the mouths of politicians.

Respect is the highest degree of accomplishment. Respect can only be earned over a period of time. You might like some, enjoy their company, even consider them your friend or lover, but to truly love someone, you must respect that person.

Say what you mean and do what you say. This will give you the highest reward from your fellow peers—respect. We all listen to a person's words, but we give their actions more value.

19) *"Dreams are as real as we make them, and the more we believe in them, the more attainable they become."*

Belief is what motivates us to action. Everyone has beliefs. It is those beliefs that separate one from another. The environment and people we associate with ingrain our beliefs into us.

These beliefs are fed to us by others and become a part of us, but we have the ability to add another dimension to how we grow and advance by implementing our own new beliefs.

Dreams or imagination will help us attain goals in life. This includes health as well as any other goals we want to accomplish. There are no goals without first having a dream, from the safety pin to the computer all started with a dream. Not necessarily the ones that occur during sleep mode but the ones we have while conscious.

We all dream of different things or situations or accomplishment we would like to accomplish. Dreams by themselves are not enough. Without true belief in your ability to accomplish these dreams it's not happening.

Every successful person reached their goal in life by believing that their dreams are as real as we make them but the more we believe in them the more attainable they become.

20) *"Gather all the wisdom of the universe as we travel through space and time and make it a part of our journey here on this planet."*

The way we gather wisdom is measured in time; intelligence we are born with. Consequently, we can only gain wisdom from the past. Everything we hear, do, or see adds to our wisdom. If we had to rely on our own short stay on this planet, there would not be enough time to gather the necessary wisdom.

In order to broaden and expand on our wisdom, it is necessary to go back in history, as we do that we are traveling backward through space and time.

If we could gather all the wisdom of the universe as we travel through space and time and make it part of our journey here on this planet, we would expand upon our wisdom not only through real life experiences but also through experiences of our predecessors.

Wisdom is the ultimate power.

21) *"Hurt can only occur if there is intent; otherwise it is a misperception."*

The spoken word is a powerful tool. A word could put one into a rage, a word could make you laugh, cry, or even have you fall in love.

Theoretically, all words have dictionary meanings, but the meanings themselves are sometimes ambiguous. When we put a sentence together with all the many words and all of their individual meanings now we are interpreting a total sentence not a word. One sentence can now be interpreted using a second method other than the "meaning," tone of voice, facial expressions, physical actions etc.

How you interpret what you hear and do what you see will determine your response.

Countless amounts of harm can come from misinterpretation. Families split, best friends fight, and people even kill according to how they interpret the spoken word.

It's factual that a good percentage of these misfortunes were born from misinterpretation of what was said and, more importantly, what one really meant by the giver as a misconception by the receiver.

In many cases, we say things and others misinterpret it, which leads to misconception. One can only hurt another when there is intent to do so. Hurt can only occur if there's intent; otherwise it is a missed perception.

22) *"Man is a computer. His brain is the processor. Alter the processor and you change the man."*

The computer is one of the most complex pieces electronic equipment created.

It is programmed by thousands of different brains throughout the world. It stores information on almost any subject one can think of. The information we receive is only as good as the brain that programmed it. It could not differentiate between right or wrong; it just spits out what was put in it. However, if we find what was programmed to be wrong, we use the same information to reprogram the information in, so the information that comes out changes.

From birth to death, our brains are programmed by many other brains (humans). We learn from our surroundings. We become a culmination of all our programming. We are not always programmed properly and sometimes suffer because of it.

Consider yourself a computer that has been programmed by other brains throughout your life.

If you don't like what was put in, reprogram your own brain to change the results.

Humans are computers. Their brain is the processor. Alter the processor (brain) and you change the human.

23) *"The heartless man said, 'You will lose much sleep if you loan money to friends and unknowns.' The caring man said, 'I will lose more if I do not.'"*

When I used the term *money*, I am also referring to other niceties as well. Every one of us are always in a position to help someone in need. Other people's needs are often not only monetary.

Help comes in many forms. It could be as simple as a donation some of your time to a meeting, performing chores for the elderly and helpless, etc.

What we do for others is a product of how we feel about ourselves. Many people are mean spirited and try to spread their selfishness to others.

Humility is a key to life. If we have no need or desire to help our fellow man, then we live in total selfishness, heartlessness. The heartless man says you will lose much sleep if you lend money to friends; the caring man said I will lose much more if I don't.

24) *"It is unfortunate that the wisdom of the aged cannot be transferred to the recklessness of youth."*

Standing on the sideline, we are watching two cars coming at each other, but there is nothing we can do to prevent the crash. We know it's going to happen before it actually does, but there is no way to communicate that to the two drivers.

The main conflicts between parents and children are all based on the difference of our wisdom. Wisdom is a culmination of life experiences. It is not expected to be as mature in our youth as in our elders; as hard as we try, there is no satisfactory way to communicate our knowledge. Youth in humans as well as animals have their own agenda and must continue to fumble while learning what we already know.

It is unfortunate that the wisdom of the aged cannot be transferred to the reckless of our youth.

25) *"Evil rots the core of society."*

Evil takes on many forms and is displayed in a myriad of ways.

There is no good that comes from evil for evil has no redemption.

It is amazing how man can take on so many different complex personalities. The worst of which is evil.

Fortunately, the percentages of evil are in the minority, but they affect the majority.

Evil sends fear through the lives of many. It kills our loved ones; it destroys neighborhoods and brings down nations while slaughtering millions.

Evil is like a plague. It starts off small but eventually evil rots the core of society.

26) *"The eye cannot see what the heart feels."*

Seeing is only a portion of reality. The emotional part of a person is invisible. We make decisions on situations or feelings about people permanently on what we see.

We all know what we see is not always what you get because the eyes cannot see what the heart feels.

27) *"The other man's success is only an image that reality can shatter."*

Success is such an ambiguous word. We measure it using a different barometer. Unfortunately, we tend to measure other people's success by their positions and their lifestyle.

People knowing that is how they are perceived tend to camouflage the truth. In order to boost their ego in the eyes of others, they surround themselves with items of expense such as labels, furs, cars, etc.

It is a well-known fact that many of the people who display bling really can't afford their lifestyle.

It is only a matter of time till the ego gets the best of us, and the lifestyle comes tumbling down like a deck of cards.

Their entire life was built on a false foundation just to impress others until realizing reality caught up to them the other man's success is only an image that reality can shatter.

28) *"The ability to achieve is as limitless as your ability to imagine."*

Imagination, dreams, wishing—all have the same connotation. Without an image, we have no goal; and with no goal, we can't achieve.

From the simplest things to the most complex, nothing happens without an image. Many of our images are of simple everyday chores. However, when we press our imagination and create very clear images of what we want, the ability to achieve is as limitless as your ability to imagine.

29) *"When the heart is empty, we are alone."*

By nature, humans like animals travel in packs. No matter how social one may be, there is more to life than things and friends.

We often hear the saying, "He died from an empty heart." Self-satisfaction is a goal we all wish to achieve. Without inner peace, we have nothing. Many people fight relationships; some through fear, others through ignorance.

When we speak of the heart in these terms, not medical terms, we are referring to emotions.

Love is an emotion and can take on many categories—the love of an animal, the love of a hobby, the love of music and art, and the love of the family.

We never know what is inside the seemingly happy-go-lucky individual who is being the life of the party but no matter what it looks like from the outside, if his heart is empty, he is alone.

> 30) *"To live only in the world and not the imagination is to waste God's gift to us."*

Reality is the disappointing side of imagination. To imagine and to dream a goal is a gift the deeper, and the more frequently we use our imagination, the more successful we will become remember when you imagine everything is perfect but reality rarely is.

> 31) *"Stupidity is most dangerous when we will not admit to it."*

We often hear people referring to others as stupid. No one is totally stupid. Ignorance and stupidity are quite different from each other. In fact, all of us are ignorant from time to time.

According to the dictionary, ignorance is being uninformed, unaware, lack of information on a particular subject. We are all ignorant when it comes to a particular happening (uninformed). However, if we are explained by somebody of knowledge as to the subject matter of what the facts are and still refuse to accept them, that is stupidity. Stupidity is the lack of reason or rejection of what is common knowledge.

When we are presented with the facts or the truth or the bigotry of our actions and refuse to capitulate, we are acting out of stupidity, which always ends up being hurtful to others. Stupidity is most dangerous when we will not admit to this.

32) *"Friendship is based on a perception of what is; only in time of need is the true measure of friendship known."*

We'll go through life having friends, acquaintances, and cliques. The chemistry created between individuals will determine the category they fall into. Friends form a more intimate relationship with each other then do acquaintances or clicks.

Some of those friendships last for years and the relationship almost becomes incestuous. Friends form lifetime bonds doing everything together from family functions to vacations.

During all of this partying, socializing, and practically living together, neither of the parties were ever in real need. At that point, all is perception. Need will bring reality. Friendship is based on perception of what is. Only in time of need is the true meaning of friendship known.

33) *"Love scorned is attacked by ego and emotion, and emotions have no brain."*

Weddings—two blissful people walking down the aisle displaying their unbridled love for each other while their families and friends share in their happiness and love that they have for each other.

Time goes by and life takes a toll on all of us. Pressure we create turns into stress and this stress changes who we are.

The love and passion we shared is being replaced by animosity and eventually the blissful couples are now in divorce court.

In most of these cases, one or both parties have had their ego attacked. Attack one's ego and emotions begin to flair. This is true not just in marriage but in any relationship between two people. Our emotions turn to hate and a need to conquer at any cost, even using children as weapons, mass destruction through brainless acts.

Love scorned is attacked by ego and emotions have no brains.

34) *"If God created what man can overcome, can God be among the living?"*

Mountains, hurricanes, earthquakes, tornadoes, blizzards, even plagues, all a part of nature, and forgetting religions for a moment; considered by most to be created by God.

The most miraculous thing about man is the ability to overcome all these and many other obstacles put before us.

People made it to the top of Mount Everest. Hurricane communities built flood walls. Architects and engineers designed structures to withhold against earthquakes. People even gave us the ability to fly.

We have proven through history that we have the ability to survive, achieve, and conquer things that nature has dealt us. Not all of us can accomplish these achievements only a select few. Most of us are the recipients of their genius.

If God created what man can overcome, can God be amongst the living?

35) *"Listening to the problems of others trivializes our own, but really helps to change or comfort us."*

I have talked about people's problems, which I like to refer to as life situations to be handled.

We allow these problems (situations) to consume our life. To us, they are so devastating that we can't enjoy the most important gift—peace.

If we took time to compare our situations with those of the world, at the moment we realize how good we really have it. The problem is we don't know how to accept the blessings we have even after listening to others.

We walk away from others in complete disarray of what they are facing, and in many cases, thank God it is not ourselves. Within minutes, we are again agonizing over our own situation.

Listening to the problems of others trivializes our own but really helps to change or comfort us.

36) *"One's desires cannot come before one's needs."*

Many of us think we know what that means, but the selfish side of the human will not allow us to see the truth.

We are born with desires. We are also born with the ability to practice self-restraint. The stronger of the two will prevail and that will determine who we really are.

Desires are costly, not only referring to money but to relationships.

Needs are that which require one to provide food, roof, education, time, and love to our family. Any interfering with that should not be acceptable.

How often do we let our desires, sometimes nefarious ones, interfere with our needs? More than one would admit. We all give into our desires and that is fine, in fact necessary to keep a normal balance. It's not the doing, and what it is that you are doing. If what you are doing to satisfy your desires, interfere with your needs, problems follow.

One's desires cannot come before one's needs.

37) *"Love comes in many packages. It's the wrapping that attracts but the content that is meaningful."*

Love is often a misconception of one's true being, and it often begins with the typical attraction to one another. In the beginning, that package is a beautiful gift, which comes beautifully wrapped. However, unwrapping that said package and looking on the inside is what will determine true love.

38) *"Program your processor with positive power and see the results."*

Our brain is like a computer's processor. If you don't like the information coming out, then reprogram it so the information going in is now positive and now the information coming out will be changed to positive.

39) *"To love is to enjoy the pleasures of one another."*

To truly love, there must be a deep respect shown between two people. That respect has to be earned through deeds performed, and the quality of the life you lead. Once that is accomplished and you have attained true love, then all the time you spend together will be a quality experience.

40) *"Believe in what you see, but what you see is an image of what you believe."*

Looking at objects, studying a piece of art, and watching a street confrontation are all brain-and-eye coordination.

The eyes will transmit an image to the brain and the brain will interpret what it saw. Surprisingly, others looked at the same thing you did, but their brain interpreted it differently.

How can people looking at the same thing see it differently? This is because what you see is an image that has been interpreted by a different brain thereby producing a different image this is what makes eyewitnesses to situations contradict each other.

Believe in what you see. What you see is an image of what you believe.

41) *"We are all born with love; we learn about evil."*

Babies come out crying, but it doesn't take long for that smile to appear while in its mother's arms being loved.

There comes a time when this baby will begin to see and interpret what it sees. At that age, it can't distinguish between love and evil, good or bad. We just interpret that which we see. As we grow, we react to the things we saw.

If we see things while growing, we mimic them in life, not differentiating between right and wrong, and if the things we see are evil, we have been damaged by our teachings.

We are born with love; we learn about evil.

42) *"Praying is a form of imagery since what we are praying for is not yet attained."*

We may not realize how much we use imagery while conducting everyday activities. Without the use of imagery, we would be unable to accomplish our goals.

Imagery sets up a picture of our desires. As the image, it's clear; it becomes a reality in our mind. The clearer your picture, the closer the reality.

When we pray, we are asking for something that at the present we don't have, but our mind has an image of the results.

Praying is a form of imagery since what we are asking for is yet to be attained.

43) *"A good reader is a good learner. There are experts that say, 'Give me a good reader and the rest is easy.'"*

Reading gives one the opportunity to experience through their imagination the history of our world through the eyes of others and adds another dimension to our wisdom going forward without the ability to read one can only learn from their experiences, which will lead to a very shallow life

44) *"Failure and success are states of mind; therefore, you are neither until you decide you are."*

Failure can be the other side of success. Our journey through life is going to be met with many roadblocks, disappointments, and setbacks. Any of these obstacles can throw us into failure if we allow it to. It depends if you are ready to give up or continue to fight—all mind-set. Success is an individual measurement. No matter what you have accomplished in life, only you can determine what success is achieved. Remember, failure and success are states of mind therefore you are either until you decide you are.

45) *"Life is like a boomerang; whatever you throw out there will always return."*

What we must understand about our life, who we become, how others treat us, our relationships with family and friends, the level of respect we get in the business world and all other phases of our everyday living, is a total culmination of what we do to shape the image of who we are.

QUOTES

Everything we do, everything we say, every action you take, including what we don't do or don't say or actions we don't take have a direct effect on who we are and how we are perceived. How others perceive us has a profound effect on all of us.

We all know when we flip the boomerang, according to the force we use, it will travel through out the atmosphere at any point Flip it's direction and is returned to sender. What we must realize is every word we speak every action we take no matter how trivial will travel from person to person through the same atmosphere. Sometimes we do such small, what we consider trivial, wrongs that no one will ever notice.

We must begin to realize that everything we say or do is going to be interpreted by someone. How it is interpreted by who is how it will come back and in what form and strength. Yes, life is a boomerang; whatever you throw out, there will always be a return.

Notes

Notes

Notes

Printed in the USA
CPSIA information can be obtained
at www.ICGtesting.com
JSHW080237170924
69814JS00001B/51